LEADERSHIP
THE NEVER-ENDING STORY

For a complete list of Global Management titles, visit our website at www.goglobalmgt.com or email us at infoGME@aol.com

LEADERSHIP
THE NEVER-ENDING
STORY

Paul Bridle

**Published in 2009 by Global Management Enterprises, LLC.
Massachusetts, USA**

ISBN 978-1-934747-56-8

Contents

Introduction

What do Leaders *do* that makes them leaders?

I want to share with you one of the great realizations I have discovered in my life as a basis for being able to answer this question.

With just about everything we learn in our life, we are taught there is the "right way of doing it." However, I have also discovered that the right way is not always the way we end up doing it, but we still get the same results.

Let us take some examples. When we were taught to drive, we were told how to hold the wheel, how to turn the wheel, and many other rules and techniques for driving. All of them were perfectly valid and made sure we were in control of the car and drove carefully. My question is, how many of us drive like that today? We don't hold the wheel in the same way and – I don't know about you – but I certainly don't turn the wheel in the way I was taught!

This concept was reinforced for me one day when I attended a speech by an MP, given to a group of young businessmen and women in the community. I had been on a number of Presentation Skills courses that told you how to stand, never to turn your back on the audience (particularly when speaking), how to use a flipchart or an overhead projector and many other rules for giving a good presentation or speech. This MP was a brilliant speaker. He wowed his audience and kept them amused for nearly an hour with a very timely and interesting presentation. However, as I watched him, I noticed that he was breaking all the rules I had been taught.

He sat on the edge of the table while he spoke to us. He turned his back on us and continued to speak to us while he was writing on the whiteboard. He didn't follow the structure of a presentation and didn't use cards for his notes! Yet, despite this, he was one of the best speakers I had seen at that time – and he not only got over his message but he also did it in a way that took us all along with him and made it enjoyable.

So my point is this. A lot of the rules or requirements that you find in good management books or are taught in business schools are absolutely correct (in the same way that holding the wheel of the car in the ten-to-two way is correct) but these rules are not always the way to get the results your require.

 Sometimes rules are at their best when they are understood and then broken.

In fact, I find that great leaders often break all the rules and taboos we find in schools and books. So why do we have rules? I have started to realize that these rules are generally put there for the following reasons:

1. to provide the learners with a basis to get through the learning phase

2. to provide the learners with a discipline or a framework to work from

3. to satisfy the teacher that the learners understood what was said and could apply it.

All of these are valid reasons for learning what we learn. However, the truth is that the rules are not set in stone.

So, as we go through this book, I will present things to you as I found them when I spoke to leaders and the people who work for leaders. What I hope you discover is their way of interpreting the rules.

In all cases, they understood the principle behind the particular rule and made sure that this was adhered to. For example, the MP who spoke to us all those years ago recognized that the rule which said "don't turn your back on the audience when speaking to them" was in place because if you do that, the audience won't be able to hear you quite as well as if you were facing them. So, he compensated for this by projecting his voice and increasing the volume a little whenever he turned around to write on the flipchart. I am sure that if he was not capable of projecting his voice so well, then he would not have spoken with his back to us at any stage.

As a means to help us to learn how to speak, the rule is a good one. It also acts as a reminder that if we break this rule we need to compensate in some way so that the people at the back can still hear us. When we undergo training, we need to demonstrate to the person teaching us that we have learnt the rule and so probably will be heard by everyone when speaking.

In the case of leaders, they are good at adapting the rules, but on the basis of (a) understanding the principle and then (b) compensating when breaking the rule. As you read the book, please notice the principle behind the rules and how leaders compensate so as to achieve the success they do.

1

The Importance of a Leader

Today is different. There has never been a day like it before. Tomorrow, the world will change again. New technology will be invented. New patents will be logged. We will have to adapt our ideas again. Where once we could hide behind the premise that "you can't teach old dogs new tricks," nowadays if you don't learn new tricks, your progress becomes short-lived.

Closures of shipyards, coal mines and other heavy industry have forced us to rethink how we earn a living and keep the United States among the top economies. Resistance to change has impeded this process, but change has happened. You only have to look at the scene around New York, Peoria and Kansas City to see that, in spite of protestations at the time, people have adapted. Now we are more ready for change. The closure of major manufacturing plants across the country might bring strident protests from the unions, but even on the days when they are announced, government officials and local councilors are already talking about gearing up to bring about different types of jobs for the workforce that is about to become unemployed. It seems we are learning the lesson.

Over the last 100 years, the rate of change has gradually become faster and faster. The concept of dictatorship as a form of management started to disappear with the introduction of unions and legislation to prevent the worst excesses of profit-hungry industrial magnates. Advertising and marketing have become increasingly sophisticated. We decided that our industries would run better if we managed rather than dictated. This certainly improved matters, but didn't eliminate many of the challenges we faced.

But what of leaders and leadership? If we go back through history, we are more likely to think of politicians, generals or admirals as being people who were considered the great leaders of their time. During more recent decades, we have had great entrepreneurs who are considered leaders in their field, such as Henry Ford – but have they really been renowned for being leaders of men?

Manager or Leader?

Perhaps to understand this distinction fully, we need to consider the exact difference between a **manager** and a **leader**. There are a great many definitions that seek to highlight the difference between the two. Let us look at this more closely.

A manager is there to fulfill a task or manage a specific area of work. A manager is responsible for allocating tasks to the various team members, ensuring that the budget is adhered to, the targets are met, rules and regulations are kept to and progress is fully reported.

Above all, the manager has to have good organizational ability to achieve the task. This manager may well have learned in management school how to do this. A manager will understand the following:

- **Objectives** – the need to know what is to be achieved

- **Knowledge** – having the understanding and wisdom to be able to do it

- **Ability** – having the right skills and competence to do what is required

- **Parameters** – knowing how far to go before referring to higher authority

- **Evaluation** – knowing how achievements are going to be measured.

These factors are important and managers need to have them clearly in mind. Many managers also believe that this is all they need to give to people who work for them.

However, there are probably occasions when you have delegated a task to a team member and have carefully considered all the above factors. As a result, you confidently expected the task to be done by the deadline set. However, when that deadline is upon you, you find that the person has not even started the task or has no hope of completing it in the time allocated.

It is at this point that many managers have a tendency to lose their patience and demand to know why the job hasn't been done. Blame is cast squarely upon the person's shoulders. So the next time, there is a considerable reluctance about delegating a task to this person. Managers have deadlines to meet and standards to uphold.

In your case, you may say that perhaps it would be better just to do it yourself rather than risk being let down again. You may even mention in conversation how this person has let you down, and now all on the management team have the image that this individual doesn't perform as required. This poor person now has an uphill task to prove being worthy of the position he or she holds.

You begin to question that management training that you went on. It obviously wasn't as foolproof as it made out and you drop back into old habits.

So what exactly is going on? 'Management,' as you have come to understand it, has not always worked for you and it's clear that something more is needed.

Having that 'something extra' makes the difference between a manager and a leader. Our thinking has evolved again, and now it is widely recognized that in industry and in commerce, just as in politics and community life, what we need is not just managers, but leaders. So we define of the difference between a manager and a leader as:

Managers manage <u>things:</u>

Leaders lead <u>people</u>

A manager manages 'things' (equipment, documentation, time, money, resources, etc.) but a leader leads people. People mostly hate being managed, but equally most people like to be led. In fact, the majority of people *want* to be led. People don't like the idea of their heads being on the chopping block, so they want someone to give them the guidance or direction. What they hate is someone standing over them telling them what to do.

What is a Leader?

In comparing a manager and a leader, we should also consider what we expect of a leader. He or she may not necessarily have organizational qualities. However, the leader is able to inspire others to achieve the task set within the deadline. Further to this, the leader seems able to inspire others with a vision of how he or she sees the future.

Norman Schwarzkopf gave an apt description of leadership when he was in command of the Allied Forces during the Gulf War.

"The challenge of leadership is to get <u>people</u> to <u>willingly</u> do more than they normally would, to rise above the norm, to perform at their higher level of potential."

It is the word 'willingly' that is so fascinating about this statement. It is easy to manage through manipulation, fear or even blackmail, to achieve short-term results from people. It is not always easy to get people to 'willingly' take action, and particularly if it is not something they necessarily want to do.

Let us be clear about what we mean by 'leadership.' We are talking about long-term, sustained motivation of people. Anyone can gain short-term commitment or motivate people to do something for a little while. It is easy. Hold a gun to their head or kidnap their families! That may sound ridiculous, apart from not being legal. Okay, in day-to-day business life, threaten them with their job or some other form of fear-based method. You will get them to do something for you using this method. However, this only works for a while. It is not sustained motivation. Leadership is the ability to get people to do something 'willingly' for a longer period of time and not just until they can find a way out of the situation.

Yes, the manager does have the big stick in the cupboard which he or she can use if people do not perform. However, now more than ever, the workforce has become more mobile, people are less worried about changing jobs and companies. This means that if a manager is not also a leader who can inspire his or her people to willingly perform at their higher level of potential, then the results will more than likely be evident in the high turnover of staff, lower staff morale and a mediocre performance.

There was an interesting survey carried out, looking at a number of companies and interviewing three tiers of employees, starting at the top. The survey asked "What motivates you and what do you think motivates your subordinates?" They asked the same questions of the middle tier, and the bottom tier. They asked "What motivates you and what do you think motivates the top person?" Here are the results:

Level 1 – Top tier

What motivates you?
1. Achievement
2. Advancement
3. Job Interest
4. Salary
5. Responsibility
6. Job Growth

What motivates your subordinates?
1. Salary
2. Advancement
3. Recognition
4. Job Interest
5. Security
6. Status

Level 2 – Middle tier

What motivates you?
1. Achievement
2. Job Interest
3. Advancement
4. Salary
5. Responsibility
6. Job Growth

What motivates your subordinates?
1. Salary
2. Advancement
3. Recognition
4. Security
5. Job Interest
6. Status

Level 3 – Lower tier

What motivates you?
1. Achievement
2. Job Interest
3. Salary
4. Advancement
5. Responsibility
6. Job Growth

What motivates your bosses?
1. Salary
2. Relation with superiors
3. Status
4. Security
5. Company policy
6. Advancement

The interesting conclusion from this was that, at every level, people are motivated more by achievement and job interest than anything else, and yet nearly all the participants assumed that everyone else was more motivated by salary. A real leader knows this and so it is the leader, rather than the manager, who has the ability to create an environment where people are more motivated, because the leader is people-orientated rather than just task-orientated.

In the 21st century, we need leaders, because management by itself is no longer enough to ensure our future.

Over the past centuries, we have seen many changes in management – and leadership – style because our environment and the ever-changing nature of life has required it. Do we now know everything there is to know about leaders and leadership? No, because the ever-changing nature of life means that our need for more and more understanding and knowledge about ourselves and how we operate and think is continuous. My book and my research combine for one step on the way. I hope that it will take your understanding of leaders and leadership to a new level, but I also hope that you will see that this is not a definitive work, because this is a never-ending story.

SUMMARY

➢ Perceptions of how to be a good boss in business have changed though time.

➢ Tasks are managed, people are led.

➢ A leader provides long-term sustained motivation of people.

➢ Having leaders is essential in the 21st Century.

➢ Our understanding of leaders and leadership will always continue to develop.

2

Breeding Successful Business

Research into leaders and leadership has led me to scrutinize successful businesses as well as those that seem to be struggling. A successful business is customer-focused and many companies have realized that customer service is a crucial factor in gaining and retaining business. So, the demand for training in customer service is high because it is believed that this will solve the problems at the interface between supplier and client. However, I have come to believe that this is starting at the wrong end of the process and can be like painting a rotten window sill. It will look better for a little while, but sooner or later, the rot will show again, this time even worse than before.

Research conducted over the last two years has identified that there are certain principles that are required within a business for long-term success. All the organizations visited and assessed showed that there were certain building blocks in place that provided a basis from which the company could, and always would, be able to develop a customer-focused business. I must point out that none of these are new to us but what is interesting is the way that they are reliant on each other.

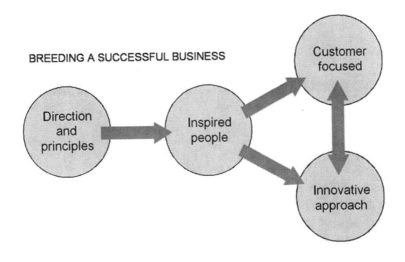

Figure 1 – Breeding a successful business

Direction and Standards

Firstly, there is the basic need for direction and standards. There is a fundamental need for the organization to know where it is going, to understand and be focused on its niche market and to know the standards it aims to achieve within that market place. The *long-term successful organizations* are focused on what they do and aim to be the best at doing it.

Inspired People

Having set this foundation, the next step is to have inspired people working for them. These successful companies and businesses put a great deal of effort into recruiting and developing their people. The extent that this is true was demonstrated many times by the policy they had of recruiting people with the right attitude and not because of the skills they could offer. As one manager explained, "I want to know that they can and <u>want</u> to smile. They don't need to know the business, because I can train them in that but it is a lot harder to train an attitude." He clarified this even more by adding, "In fact, I don't recruit from within the trade as I don't want to have any of their bad habits."

Customer Approach

Now we get to the bit about the successful business having a customer-driven approach to all they do. Never before has there been a greater need to focus on the customer – and these companies have developed this to a precise art. In an age when the product is broadly similar to the competition, in many cases the only cutting edge between competing companies is the service they offer. These companies have an approach to dealing with their customers that just makes the customers keep coming back.

What is most interesting about these steps is that each step is only possible when the previous step is in place. For example -

- Good customer approach is only possible when there are inspired people working in the business. All our research shows that it is not possible to sustain good customer service unless the philosophy within the business is first to treat colleagues and co-workers with respect and get along with each other internally.

- It is not possible to achieve a continued level of enthusiasm and inspired people when they don't know the direction and standards the business is trying to achieve.

Innovative ability

Finally, and on an equal footing with customer approach, is their innovative ability. Having set the fundamentals in place, the company is then able to be innovative in its activities, innovative about its marketing, its approach to dealings with customers, suppliers and community, innovative with the product and the business process. Once again, this innovation comes about because of the inspired people (staff are involved and are contributing with new ways of doing business) and the customer approach (listening to the customer means that the customer tells you things).

Instead of one or two managers or a paid marketing person being expected to be creative and come up with new ideas and innovative approaches, the whole company is being creative and this generates many more ideas.

In addition, because of the customer approach within the business, even the customer is responding in a similar manner by providing feedback on good practice and such matters as alternative uses for the product.

Companies that spend time trying to teach 'customer service' are starting at the wrong end of the process. Good customer service will come automatically from inspired people who enjoy a culture of getting on with each other first. Equally, the people will be inspired as a result of the company instilling its direction and standards into employees so that they are motivated to move towards the vision.

Any activities that limit the above steps need to be carefully managed. For example, installing systems when trying to conform to ISO9000 can have a negative effect on people, which in turn affects the approach to the customer and will also limit the innovative ability of the company. Systems such as these need to be installed without damaging the important process of ensuring the focus is clear, the people remain inspired, everyone is customer-centered and the organization continues to seek innovative ways of growing the business.

 Thus, successful business starts from the top and is driven by leadership.

A leader gives direction and standards, creates inspired people whose enthusiasm for the business leads to an innovative approach to the business and also gives employees a natural enthusiasm and flair with the customers. Customers can sense it if the service they are given is window dressing, or if it is a genuine desire to help them.

SUMMARY

➢ Leaders breed successful business

➢ Leaders provide direction and standards

➢ Leaders recruit inspired people with the right attitude

➢ The right customer approach comes from having inspired people

➢ Inspired people providing the right customer approach gives the company the ability to be innovative

3

To be a Leader – or to Have Leadership Ability?

Many of you will have participated in team-building games within your professional career. Isn't it interesting how you managed to work through to the end of the game without ever having an official leader, and yet you still managed to complete the task. Why? Does this mean that having a leader is not necessary at all?

In this context, it is leadership that is important rather than having a leader. The leadership in the team may not have been obvious because in most cases it moved between the team members as the game progressed. Leadership had been a short-term input. If the team game had been extended over days or weeks, then the situation would have probably been different and an overall leader would be needed – and would probably have emerged.

So we start to see that there is a real and distinct difference between being a leader and having leadership. Let's consider this leadership aspect more closely. We can use the example of 'being a friend' and 'being friendly.' A friend is something you are, it is part of you and starts within you to project itself outward. You don't practice it, you don't turn it off and then on again, you simply are a friend. This is different from being friendly. We can be friendly with someone but not be their friend.

We can view leaders and leadership in the same way. Like the natural aspect of being a friend, being a leader is something you are and not something you do. A true leader is never anything but just a leader of people. A leader is about 'being' and not doing. Hence a leader starts from within and projects out. This is why they have integrity with most people and can develop it easily. The ability to gain integrity comes from the person within and not because of something he or she can do on a temporary basis. People can see through something that is put on and something that is part of that person.

This is different from the person who wants to gain integrity and so works 'on' it without reference to his or her inner self. This person is not a true leader, even though providing leadership when required, just as someone can be friendly or turn on the charm when required.

To highlight the difference between the role of a leader and leadership, let me use an example. A team of people need to get from position 'A' to position 'B.' To get there, they will require a navigator. The team's leader will transfer the leadership of the team to the person who can navigate. This person takes leadership because of his or her skills and everyone follows this person because of those skills. However, part way between 'A' and 'B,' the team comes across a river. They need to build a bridge to cross the river. The team leader will now give the leadership to the engineer. The engineer has the skills to get the team forward from this point. While the engineer has the leadership role, everyone will follow this person's instructions to build a bridge. Having built the bridge and crossed the river, the leadership will move to another person with particular skills needed depending on the demands of the next phase of the journey.

This analogy is effective in showing the difference between the leader and having the role of leadership. First note that the leader remains the leader throughout the journey. However, he or she will hand over the leadership to the best person to help the team move forward at any time. Normally that leadership comes in the form of expertise they have. True leaders are always seeking to give away leadership but they still maintain the position of leader. They see giving away leadership as an important part of getting the most out of people.

A leader will obviously provide 'leadership.' However, true leaders recognize two things about themselves: firstly, their ability to lead must ultimately come from within and, secondly, that they are not always the best people to give leadership (even when they are the leader of the team or group).

Let's examine these in more detail:

1. **The Leader from within**

   A leader must have certain attributes and a mind-set or frame of mind. We will discuss these attributes in this book. It is this combination of certain attributes and mind-set or frame of mind that makes a true leader. For example, a leader knows that a person is fully engaged and motivated when they are in control. When a person is truly engaged and motivated they don't rely on any external force. They are in control and will seek ways to achieve their aims by using resources around them rather than relying on external influences to motivate them to get things done. This is what we call self-leadership. So a true leader is always seeking to develop 'self-leadership' for their people rather than trying to lead them.

2. **Giving away leadership**

   Building on the above, because leaders are not trying to lead (since they are 'being' a leader), they recognize that leadership must and will move away from them. So, in particular circumstances, they will give leadership away to whoever can provide it best at any particular moment. Nevertheless, the leader is still there to provide encouragement, support and direction if needed.

So we can see why the team-building games are successful. Leadership has passed through various hands at various times. Whoever has taken on the short-term mantle of leadership, has had certain skills or ability which the team recognize is needed to take them forward. However, what would happen if they were to continue to operate as a team for an indefinite period of time?

What happens if we extrapolate this example?

Now the team know each other better, Jack knows that Harry is excellent at providing creative ideas to accomplish their projects. But now Jack is reluctant to help Harry every time he requests it because of the arrogant way in which Harry expects others to fall into line. Harry starts fancying himself as the boss of the team. Jack is also pleased with the way that Sue always takes care of the financial details and often pulls them up before they go into a loss-making situation. However, Jack and Harry are getting irritated by the way that Sue never lets them know details so that they can plan ahead. She guards her job and the information and won't give away more than she needs, for fear of losing control. Sue and Harry are pleased that Jack always takes charge of implementing the plans, but sometimes he just cannot take a decision. He would dither, with the result that the team has become frustrated with him. Quite soon, the team gradually falls apart. What started out as a successful team starts to falter.

While recognizing and acknowledging the leadership that each brings to the team, there is an overall feeling of dissatisfaction and lack of achievement. Because none of the team members is a true leader and although each was capable of taking leadership, they could not sustain the momentum in the long term.

I have seen similar situations with voluntary community organizations such as Lions Club, Rotary and Kiwanis. Each local branch has a president for one year and it is possible to see where there are true leaders taking office. These are the branches that steam ahead during the year, where the team is cohesive and is working towards the vision of the president. They achieve wonderful projects and recruit new members.

At the end of the year, the branch is riding high. There are other presidents, however, who are not true leaders, but offer leadership. They continue doing what has been done before, they are steady, willing to work hard, offer integrity and in doing so, keep the branch ticking over without particularly moving the branch forward with direction and focus.

Unless a true leader takes control, each year will see a slow deterioration of the branch until it will eventually cease to exist. In these cases, the membership becomes disillusioned and leaves because nobody is coordinating the leadership ability of the members as well as providing the abilities of a leader.

The same scenario is also played out in companies – for example, retail companies. They have virtually identical shops in a number of towns selling the same products, with the same layout of store, the same training program for staff, the brand image, and serving the same market sector. I have seen some stores performing consistently at a very much higher level than their equivalent in the next town, serving a similar demographic population. The reason lies with the person at the top, the leader.

Jaguar cars is an example. Ten years ago it was losing vast amounts of money. Ford took it over, but the interesting part of this is that the turn around happened with the existing workforce. A true leader was appointed. New values were instilled, the greatest of these being respect for each other and respect for the experience that many employees had built up over many years. The leader passed leadership to these employees.

Further difference between a true leader and having a leadership role can be clearly seen in times of hardship or crisis. A true leader will tend to be able to ride out the storm, stand by the integrity he or she has built up with the employees and, by allowing leadership to move to others, the best will be made of the situation. Someone who has a leadership role and is not prepared to pass it around, will often start to panic, and behave irrationally because he or she is afraid of losing control. Often such an individual's answer is to produce petty rules to bring about some control. Employees will then spend more time complaining about restrictions imposed upon them, than being focused on what they are meant to be doing.

 So being a leader is not about taking control. It is about *being* in control enough to give the leadership away and encourage the leadership within others.

If a person feels the need to control, he or she has lost the ability to lead. An employee who is well motivated by the leader will have no problem in governing his or her own job, and will not want to be bound by silly rules. Having such petty rules imposed as a means of taking control will only serve to tell the employees that they are not trusted, and all the "leader's" integrity that may have been built up will disappear in one easy move. Taking control is out of place and is a restrictive management practice that has no place in the thinking of a modern leader.

SUMMARY

➤ *Being a leader* is something that comes from within.

➤ *Leadership* is a temporary role based normally on a skill or expertise.

➤ Leaders give away leadership.

➤ Leaders encourage self-leadership.

➤ Leaders learn the principle behind the rule and not just the rule.

4

What Makes a Leader?

If we always do what has always been done, and tread the path of least resistance, then life is easy. However, it offers no new opportunities and gives no hope for the future. If there is to be any galvanizing of the forces towards achieving something different from the norm, then there is the need for leaders.

So great is the importance of leaders to ensure that we breed successful 'organizations,' and yet we are in a situation where there are fewer and fewer leaders in industry, commerce, government, schools and social groups and more and more books and training courses on the subject. Much of what we read on Leadership is excellent material, but people find it hard to put it into practice and it is often difficult to measure progress.

I spoke to many that had attended training sessions of various types. They had all enjoyed the experience and believed that they had gained much. However, when I tackled them on how they had improved their leadership as result of these activities, they were unable to quantify the benefit. They could recite the notes they had been given and even explain the theory they had been taught, but when pushed to explain how they had put the material into effect, they would invariably start to say that their circumstances were different and it was not that easy in the real world.

This led me on a quest to find a method of explaining leadership and showing people how to develop the ability not only of leadership, but of being a leader in a measurable way. I defined a leader as someone who enabled people to follow him or her willingly, and achieved results through these people. I thought the answer I was looking for would lie in being able to enter the mind of a leader and see the world through his or her eyes and understand the way he or she thinks. With this in mind, I began visiting leaders and asking them questions that I hoped would unravel their thinking and provide me with the key I was looking for.

Rapidly I started to discover that although this was interesting and even powerful, what I was really after they did not know at their conscious level. They gave me what they thought they were doing, but on some occasions, I would speak to their staff, only to find out that what the leaders thought they were doing that made them into leaders was nowhere near the same thing that the staff respected them for or were motivated by. The more I thought about it, the more I decided what I really wanted to know was:

What does the leader *do* that inspires these people to follow?

In particular, I wanted to know what worked in the difficult times as well as the easy times, and then, could it be defined in a manner that people could be trained in – and their progress measured.

I decided that if I was going to understand what the leader does to motivate his or her staff, I needed to speak to the staff and not just the leader.

When the initial research was completed and the material was presented back to one particular leader and his team, the team was delighted with the manner of the findings. However, the leader sat nonplussed and simply said, "But everyone does that, don't they?" This was typical of the response and explains why the leaders couldn't provide the answers I was looking for. What they did that inspired people was deeper than they understood of themselves and in some cases simpler than they appreciated.

In trying to understand the role of a leader, we need to bear in mind that the leader's priority must be to achieve the task. In military terms, it may be to defeat the enemy; in business it may be to achieve a position in the market or a level of profitability; in politics it may be to achieve a level of prosperity for the country, and so it goes on. All of these are objectives that need to be achieved and out of them a number of other objectives arise.

The great John Adair recognized how important it is for the leader to keep a balanced focus. He pointed out the importance of being able to balance the focus between the needs of the task, the needs of the team and the needs of the individual. All three aspects are important and there are dangers when allowing any one to dominate the other for prolonged periods of time.

The importance of keeping this balanced focus can be likened to riding a bicycle. While riding, one needs to be aware of the bicycle and how it is performing, the condition of the road, and what is up ahead and what is coming from behind. Focus on one for prolonged periods of time can result in problems of disastrous consequences. However, this understanding is not enough to enable someone to be a good cyclist.

In everything we do there is a need for three distinct attributes. These attributes are:

- an **understanding** or a **knowledge**

- a developed **skill**

- the correct **attitude** or frame of mind.

In the example of riding the bike, we need the knowledge of which are the pedals, brakes, gears, etc. as well as some basic understanding of what is possible or correct to do in given circumstances. We also need the skills, which is the actual ability to ride the bike by pedaling, steering and maintaining balance. Finally, we need the correct attitude if we are to be able to ride safely without being a danger to ourselves and others. For example, if a person has the attitude that a cyclist should always have the right of way, then they will have problems sooner or later.

In the case of being a leader, unlike probably any other activity, the situation requires less reliance on skill or even knowledge, and greater emphasis on attitude. Of course, there is the need for knowledge, as we shall see later, but the practical application of that knowledge is based on the attitude of the person in that position. It is for this reason that we have struggled for so long to define how to be a leader.

What are the characteristics that make a leader?

Research has allowed me to talk to hundreds of people about the leaders that inspire them. I recorded and analyzed the responses I got in an effort to establish what it was a leader did that made them a leader.

When responding, people used words and short sentences to describe to me the attributes that they thought were important. I delved deeper when given answers that were too general. For example, a common answer was a 'good communicator.' So, I would endeavor to challenge what they meant by good communicator. They would then come up with explanations such as 'a good listener, 'good at keeping everyone informed,' 'good at making everyone feel they knew what was going on,' 'spoke clearly and in simple terms,' 'looked at you when he or she spoke to you,' 'made you feel that everything you said was important,' 'open stance' and many more similar expressions.

You can do this same exercise for yourself or together with others. Visualize in your mind's eye someone that you particularly admire as a leader. Someone that you feel would make a good leader or you felt happy to work for in your life. Now think carefully about this person or these people. What is it about them that inspired you or commanded enough respect from you to follow? What was their approach to life, people, work, problems and circumstances?

Contradictory Words

In certain cases, words were used that could have been defined as aggressive, and so I sought clarification to establish the underlying meaning or basis for the comment or word used. For example, 'determined' was used a few times. When asking them to expand or explain their choice of words they responded with: 'knowing which way to go,' 'clear objectives,' 'a sense of purpose' or 'knowing what was going to be achieved.'

My concern was that I would get contradictory information if some of these words were not checked for further understanding. I tested words like 'determination' against other words also given to me like 'caring,' 'considerate,' 'interested,' etc. In every case, participants were quick to point out that by being determined, it did not mean this negated the other attributes but rather that they added to it. We all use the same words but the exact meaning we attach to the words does vary from person to person.

In the case of being determined, it added strength to the situation, and their determination was a strength to their people and not seen as something to fear. In fact, it seemed that it was their ability to be determined while remaining caring and understanding about their people that set them apart. On one occasion, 'tough' was used and I sought similar clarification. They explained that it involved 'strength of character' along with 'determination.' The same individual listed 'empathy' and 'concerned about people' as characteristics of the leader.

Mr. or Mrs. Perfect

As more and more information was gleaned, it started to create questions in my mind. Was it was possible for one person to have all these attributes? Was I wasting my time? Was I trying to find Mr. or Mrs. Perfect? Was it really possible for one person to have all these traits?

Having spoken to hundreds of people and extracted thousands of words, I was left with the feeling that maybe I was not going to find the answers I was looking for. When I started to examine the words, it struck me that some of these were similar. It was noticeable that a pattern was emerging and so I started to group words together that were connected.

I also looked for words or expressions that were used consistently. I wasn't after what *some* people thought a leader needed but rather what *everybody* believed that a leader needed. What I found was that there were five distinct categories of characteristics that successful leaders possess. I had anticipated that I would have very many groups and was surprised that it came down to only five.

The five groups covered all the information that had consistently been provided. They also provided five headings that, once understood, could be used as measurement for people wishing to develop the ability to be a leader. Far from being a 'one off' measurement of skills, it became clear that the five headings could be used to measure ability on an ongoing basis.

Having used these headings as a measuring tool, it became possible to use it also as a training tool to highlight those areas of leadership that most needed attention in each individual. The ability to use this leadership model as a measuring tool on an ongoing basis, has taken the study of leadership, and perhaps more importantly, knowledge of how to be a leader, to the next level.

So let me take you through the five areas in broad terms and then we will study them each in more detail later in the book.

The Five Characteristics

Vision

We have called the first category **Vision**. This included all the words related to the future such as:

Having a mission
Goals or Goal orientated
Visionary
Focused
Knowing where they are going
Having direction
Committed
Innovative and entrepreneurial
Forward thinking
Courageous – bold
Audacious
Strategist
Being planners
Big picture thinking
Teleological thinking

Result-oriented

Having a clear understanding of the direction the organization is going in, is fundamental to leadership. People need to have faith that the person they are expected to follow has an understanding of the situation and the direction that is needed.

It can be most easily likened to when we are boarding a ship. We need confidence that the captain knows where we are going, and the direction and understanding that is needed to get us from here to there. It may not be the exact route because if problems arise and the route becomes blocked, the captain will need to know how to make alternative arrangements. What is needed is a captain that knows where the end is and has the ability to take us there despite the journey.

I can hear some of you saying that many voyages in history have not had a specific (known) destination and likewise today we set out not knowing where we may end up. This is also true but the voyage leader was always clear about what tasks needed to be accomplished.

This is the same with today's business and other leaders. They are required to know where to go and to have the ability to get everyone there despite the problems or difficulties that arise on the way. It is this ability to have a vision that they can articulate clearly and to provide confidence to their people, that gives the first characteristic of a leader. They are committed and believe in this vision. Their ability to comprehend the vision, see the whole picture and see all eventualities is motivational and creates confidence in others. This is not to be confused with tunnel vision, which, while extremely focused, excludes the big picture.

However, vision just by itself is not enough. If you have the chance to listen to a recording of Martin Luther King and his famous 'I have a dream' speech (try finding it on the Internet or any good CD encyclopedia), then it will make this come alive for you.

A leader is so committed to the vision that their conviction and passion is contagious. So we should relabel this section as 'Vision with Passion.'

To inspire and motivate followers requires a conviction that the vision is possible. It is not the vision itself that is contagious, it is the passion with which it is put over. Martin Luther King's vision was the equality of the races in the United States. If he had stood limply in front of the crowd that day and delivered the words 'I have a dream' in a nondescript, monotone voice, then the speech would have sunk into insignificance and I would not be writing about it today. Listening to his voice, you can feel the depth of his passion rock you, and you immediately know why he inspired the multitude of black people in America and why those opposed to equality would have reason to fear him. You also feel that when he set out on his quest to accomplish his vision, he knew it would be a long-term challenge and one that he might not even accomplish in his lifetime, but it was something he believed so passionately in, that the fight was worth starting.

Values

Values represent the second of our major categories. This covers many of the ideas of how a leader lives his or her life, and encompasses comments such as:

Integrity
Trust
Credibility
Fairness
Reliability
Keeping promises
Being committed to excellence

Honesty
Treating all people the same
Standing by you
Leading by example
Firmness

Leaders have an ability to create respect and even admiration from their people. People know where they stand with a leader and respect this feature of their abilities. Please don't confuse this with 'liking' or even 'agreeing' with him or her. This is about respecting the leader even if you do not agree or believe the same as them. This ability comes from their values. These are the standards by which the leader will live his or her life.

The leader needs to be trusted by the people that follow. To take the respect and admiration to the next level of trust requires a 'Consistent Set of Values.' It is no good for a leader to live by one set of values one day, and then by a different set of values the next. Trust comes from knowing exactly where you stand with that person and a sense of certainty that this person will act in this manner no matter what occurs. Reacting differently from day to day given a similar set of circumstances will never create respect, because people will be wary if they do not know how the leader will react. Respect will not follow, and neither will trust.

Interestingly, there's no requirement for you to like the leader. Neither does it require the leader to be law-abiding (although this does help a great deal) so long as people know where they stand with the leader. This may appear to be contradictory to the words 'honest' and 'reliable,' but think about it. History is full of leaders who were very good at galvanizing people into a common cause, and who were also ruthless and brutal, perhaps even pirates in their day. What is required is that the leaders' values are either consistent with yours, or they have values that you respect.

Of the five characteristics we will review, this is the most powerful. A real understanding of this characteristic will have the single greatest impact on being a leader. People interviewed felt that knowing where they stood with their leader was very important. A leader needed to be 'honest' with his or her people, be someone they could 'rely on' and 'depend on,' someone that was 'consistent' and even when all else failed, this was the person that could be relied on to provide a beacon of light for them to follow.

These words described the code of conduct that the leaders set for themselves. Even in cases when their people didn't agree with them, they still managed to respect them because of their standards. One of the best modern day examples of this was Margaret Thatcher. Many people did not like her, and even hated her views and her policies, but most who knew her respected her as a leader. She did not earn the title of 'Iron Lady' and make herself known for the phrase 'This lady's not for turning' for no reason. She had very rigid values and stuck by them. She was respected even if she was not liked.

Take a moment to think about managers you may have worked for. If there were any who did not have consistent values, then these were probably the ones you least enjoyed working for. At times when you took the initiative, you found that sometimes you were supported and other times berated. You may remember incidents when they asked you to do things and then denied it or blamed you for the result.

Of all the characteristics, this was the most fascinating for its ability to have a major impact on people.

People

As you can imagine, the leader's attitude towards people and the way they responded to people had a significant impact on their ability to lead. All the groups of people I interviewed confirmed this. There was so much information on their dealings with people and it covered words such as:

Being good communicators
Being good listeners
Interested
Caring
Considerate
Valuing people
Considerate
Approachable
Friendly
Patient
Thoughtful of others
Interested
Empathic
Enjoying rapport
Connecting at their level

Leaders believe and see the merit in people regardless of the position these people hold. They are good at listening to people and communicating with them. They understand communication as a two-way street. Their approach is respectful and this enables them to get on with all their people. Leaders have a real understanding of the basic needs of people, and are able to respectfully respond to those needs.

The true leader shows a real 'love' of people. We can understand many different things from the word 'love.' The Greeks in fact had seven different words for our one word 'love.'

Our love for our parents is different from the love we have for our partner, which is then different again from our love for a car, and so we can go on. In this case, our description as 'Love of People' is intended to show an attitude toward people.

It is important that this 'love' is sincere. Earlier in the book, we discussed how training people in customer service is like starting at the wrong end of the process.

How often are we met these days by someone trained in customer service at a call centre, who answers with something like: "Good morning. You're through to Widget and Company Customer Care and Help Line – Jane speaking – how may I help you?" Besides the lack of breath taken in the delivery of this introduction, it is also has the enthusiasm and sincerity of a dead fish. Sincerity is important to people.

A true 'Love of People' is in the mindset of a leader. It guides him or her naturally through all dealings with other people. Not to have this mindset would be a little like trying to use a map of Birmingham to navigate your way around London. In this example the mindset is the map of Birmingham and the situation you are tying to deal with is London.

Using the wrong map (mindset) you will get lost when trying to find your way around New York (deal with a situation). This is not New York's fault! It is your fault for using the wrong map or mindset.

So a mindset that does not appreciate people for their worth will never get the most out of those people. Love of people is a mindset about people.

Nurturing

The fourth category reflects another side to the leader's dealings with people. I have called this category 'nurturing' in as much as leaders encourage growth and development in others. The words that people used included:

Developing People
Coaching
Bringing out the best in people
Being prepared to learn
Selective people assignments
Weeding out incompetence
Encouraging others to learn
Developing a learning environment
Admitting to mistakes
Seeking opinions from others
Always giving feedback

Leaders are committed to developing people, bringing the best out of them, even when people cannot see it in themselves. They are good coaches and have the ability to identify people's strengths and move them to positions where they can use them effectively. Equally, leaders are always learning and never believe they know it all. Being a champion requires confidence in oneself, while never thinking there isn't always something new to be learnt. Leaders learn from their mistakes and help others do the same without blame.

Developing others does not mean that the leader will necessarily coach each individual but rather that the leader will ensure that each individual has the necessary training and development to enable them to grow. In the case of those closest to the leader, the leader will probably be more active in the process, always seeking to develop them and respectfully push them to new heights.

As well as developing others, good leaders have an insatiable desire to learn and a hunger for knowledge and understanding. They are also eager to share their knowledge with others. In fact, of the five characteristics, I have discovered that this one is the most important.

A leader has an insatiable desire to learn and never considers that he or she knows it all. As Rick Warren said, "The moment you stop learning, you stop leading." It is as if the leader nurtures the champion within himself or herself. I would go so far as to say that if leaders don't have this desire, then they have no basis upon which to build their ability to lead.

A true leader will not seek to cast blame for mistakes, but will endeavor to learn from them, not only for him or herself but also for others. A famous example of this is the story about Tom Watson of IBM, who reportedly was asked if he was going to fire an employee who made a mistake that cost IBM $600,000. He said, "No, why should I fire him? I just spent $600,000 training him."

There are various everyday pointers to this characteristic that you may have noticed during your working life. If there is glory to be handed out for success, then the true leader never takes the credit alone, but rather wishes his or her team to take the glory for the success. The true leader does not fear others who are gifted in similar skills, and rather than suppressing them as a threat, will be happy to encourage them to reach heights that they themselves never reached. Most of all a leader is marked by personal willingness to learn and the desire to create a learning environment.

Overview

The fifth and final characteristic is **Overview**. I was given words such as:

Empowering
Visible
MBWA (Management By Walking About)
Self motivated

Having high self-esteem
Being prepared to stay the course
Action-oriented
Developing themselves

Overview actually touched on all of the others but still needed to be set apart from the rest. I called it overview because it was described to me once that leaders need to be like a bird in a tree. This does not mean that they are above everyone – far from it, but rather that they maintain a position where they can see what is going on without getting in the way.

From a tree, I was told, the leader can see various teams working away and from that position can fly down and offer support, advice or just show interest in what is going on. However, the leader then does the most important bit, which is to get back up into the tree. It is important to be there and show interest, but it is also important to get out of the way and let people get on with what they are paid to do. In other words, leaders are visible and 'manage by walking about,' and not from behind a desk.

I was also reminded that while they were on the ground with one team, they were no longer in a position to see what the other teams were doing and whether they needed their help or not. Much later a similar illustration was given to me using a general in his helicopter. A general from his helicopter can view the movements of his troops. He can fly down and visit them, give them encouragement and tell them what is going on in other areas. He must then get out of the way and leave the commanding officer to do his job.

One of their strengths lies in empowering people and it is this empowering approach that people responded to. The leader was there for them but not doing it for them. This characteristic touched all the others in some way. Having trained or nurtured their champions, the leader would let them do the job and even allow them to make their mistakes as part of their development. Having set the vision he or she would allow people to get on with it. The clear role was to care for them and communicate with them but not do the job for them. Finally, although delegating and empowering required them to get out of the way, it did not mean becoming detached or be above anyone. In fact, they are prepared to come in at any level and provide the assistance the team needed to achieve the goals. There was nothing that was too demeaning for a leader to do. Having set the vision and standards, they viewed themselves as being there to serve and support, not stand over their people.

Wanting to take into account this ability to come in at any level when needed, I called this fifth one 'Overview with Overalls.' The leader may need to get his or her hands dirty, but just like wearing a pair of overalls, the leader can take them off and return to the overview position when the time has come. I saw a wonderful example of this when visiting a company, where the Managing Director was showing me around. We walked into the Planning Office where the team was busy at work on an urgent project that was vital for the company. The MD enquired if there was anything he could do to help. The team said they had it more or less under control and help was not needed. But as we were leaving the office one of the planners said 'All I need is a cup of tea.' Without a further word, the MD went and made tea for the whole team.

The Model

This model signifies how all the characteristics touch on each other and shows the Overview impacting on the other four characteristics. It also shows how important it is for leaders to maintain a balance between what they need to develop in themselves and in how they relate to others, with the top half representing themselves and how they live their lives (Vision and Values) and with the lower half representing how they relate to others (People and Nurturing). Equally they need to keep an eye on the present (the right hand side of Values and People), as well as the future (the left hand side of Vision and Nurturing) in all matters. Notice that the leader is not encumbered by the past.

These five characteristics summed up all the points made by all the people who answered my questions about what qualities they responded to in a leader.

What is significant is that a leader not only needs to have these qualities, but needs to demonstrate them.

- It is not enough just to have a vision – people need to be aware of the vision.

- It is not enough just to have values – they must be consistent and be seen to be consistent.

- It is not enough just to respect and value people – people need to know you respect and value them.

- It is not enough just to have the intent to nurture people – they must feel that they are being nurtured and developed.

- Empowerment and visibility cannot just happen when it suits you or when you have time – it has to be there constantly and you need to make time for it.

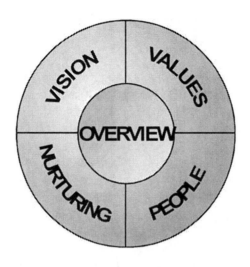

Figure 2 – The overview

We shall explore each of these attributes in more depth in the coming chapters. This will give a greater understanding and appreciation of them and the impact they have on leading people.

Summary

In everything we do, there is a need for three distinct attributes: an understanding or a knowledge, a developed skills and the correct attitude or frame of mind. For leadership the most important of these is the correct attitude or frame of mind.

The model is based on five interlinked characteristics:

> **1. Vision with Passion** - a leader needs to have a clear understanding of where he or she is going, and the passion to put this over in such a way as to inspire others.

> **2. Consistent Set of Values** - values represent the way the leader lives his or her life. Being consistent with one's values creates the integrity and respect a leader needs for others to follow willingly.

> **3. Love of People** - the leader is able to show an intense interest and empathy with others. The sincerity of this type of 'love' stems from the mindset of the leader.

> **4. Nurturing Champions** - leaders are committed to developing people and bringing out the best in them. Above all, the leader has an insatiable desire to learn.

> **5. Overview with Overalls** – the ability to delegate and empower people is characteristic of a leader. There is nothing that is too demeaning for the leader, who can provide assistance at any level, but always knows when and how to get back out of the way.

Summary (cont)

To be a leader, it is vital to demonstrate all these qualities at all times.

These five characteristics can be used to measure how you are doing against what people expect from a leader on a regular basis.

5

Vision with Passion

'The person who cannot see the ultimate,
becomes a slave to the immediate.'

Anon

In the previous chapter, we likened the leader to the captain of the ship. We have the confidence that the captain knows where we are going and the direction and understanding that is needed to get us from here to there. The above quote takes this theme one step further. I would liken the leader also to any one of us who drives a car. We get in the car with a specific destination in mind. Sometimes, on the way to our destination, we may meet a traffic jam or an accident, and we may decide to take a detour. However, our original destination does not alter and we eventually arrive, even though we may have had to overcome various obstacles on the way. If we have no ultimate destination, then our car driving is equivalent to becoming 'a slave to the immediate.' We drive around with no obvious aim, and are swayed in our driving by the immediate circumstances and in the process we waste time and resources.

Similarly, someone in a leadership position without a vision (this person cannot in my view be called a true leader) will not necessarily achieve the outcome he or she needs to or could achieve. In fact, being reactive rather than proactive may even lead to a downward spiral of events when the market or the economy changes and the managers within the company do not have the vision to move with it. It is similar to the Product Life Cycle, except that instead of a product, we are talking about the whole company. A good idea or vision may have brought the company into existence, and for a while it will make rapid increases in profit or market share. However, it reaches a plateau and after a while at the height of popularity, it will start to decline. The life cycle can be extended but will not last forever. When cornflakes were first introduced into the market, they enjoyed enormous popularity, but were later besieged by many other different cereal types, eating away at the market share. Kelloggs has extended the life cycle through various means, but if they had not had the vision to bring in completely new cereals and variations on the cornflakes theme such as Frosties, then Kelloggs as a company would probably not exist today.

On the company level, Digital is a good example how the vision of one person brought a phenomenal company into existence. For over 30 years, Digital had experienced outstanding business growth and success. However, it became blinkered to the signs of the changing market place and in 1991, Digital experienced its first ever operating loss. It took this crisis to make people take notice. They realized they had missed major windows of opportunity, had too many employees, and their products were not competitive. Corporately, they had to reduce their workforce by 50%, and the number of employees fell worldwide from 117,000 in 1990 to 62,000 in 1995. With a change in leadership, Digital has slowly been able to climb its way out of the mire, but what caused the initial downfall was the inability of the original leader to adapt his vision to the changing market place.

This gives rise to several requirements for a leader in terms of what he or she is doing INTERNALLY in the personal understanding and thinking process:

- ✍ The leader needs to think strategically, to think beyond the present, to move away from the day-to-day activities and consider the implications for the future.

- ✍ The leader needs to be able to 'step outside the box,' be objective and dispassionate when thinking.

- ✍ The leader needs to be able to look at events happening and recognize the implications for the future, i.e. have 'teleological thinking ability.'

- ✍ The leader needs to constantly reinvent the future, challenge the 'norm' and question the validity of what is being done.

I am not an advocator of writing a vision down. A vision is not a mission or purpose statement. The art of the leader is being able to take the mission or purpose and bring it to life. A vision is something that a leader uses to fire another person's imagination.

Many great leaders in our history may not have had a vision that was written down as is encouraged these days by management gurus, but the very nature of their actions can leave us in no doubt as to the nature of their vision. Perhaps the word 'great' is not always correct in this sense, because many of these leaders will go down in history as being 'infamous' rather than 'great.' Hitler's vision was to create a dominant Aryan race; Marx's vision was the equality of men, and Saddam Hussein's vision is the dominance of Iraq in the Middle East.

While others may be judged to be great rather than ultimately evil, such as Margaret Thatcher's vision to put the 'great' back into Britain, most of these leaders have suffered a downfall through not adapting their vision to current circumstances, not moving away from day-to-day activities and not considering the implications for the future.

Let us look at some of the visions of other great leaders:

Henry Ford

I will build a car for the great multitude... It will be so low in price that no man making a good salary will be unable to own one and enjoy, with his family, the blessing of hours of pleasure in God's great open spaces ...

When I'm through, everybody will be able to afford one, and everyone will have one. The horse will have disappeared from our highways, the automobile will be taken for granted and we will give a large number of men employment at good wages.

Walt Disney

The idea of Disneyland is a simple one. It will be a place for people to find happiness and knowledge. It will be a place for parents and children to spend pleasant hours in one another's company, a place for teachers and pupils to discover greater ways of understanding and education. Here the older generation can recapture the nostalgia of days gone by and the younger generation can savor the challenge of the future. Here will be the wonders of Nature and Man for all to see and understand.

Disneyland will be based upon, and dedicated to, the ideals, the dreams and hard facts that have created America. And it will be uniquely equipped to dramatize these dreams and facts and send them forth as a source of courage and inspiration to all the world.

Disneyland will be something of a fair, an exhibition, a playground, a community centre, a museum of living facts and a show piece of beauty and magic. And it will remind us and show us how to make those wonders part of our lives.

Martin Luther King

I say to you today, my friends, that in spite of the difficulties and frustrations of the moment, I still have a dream. It is a dream deeply rooted in the American dream.

I have a dream that one day the nation will rise up and live out the true meaning of its creed: "We hold these truths to be self-evident, that all men are created equal."

I have a dream that one day on the red hills of Georgia the sons of former slaves and the sons of former slave owners will be able to sit down together at the table of brotherhood.

I have a dream that one day even the state of Mississippi, a desert state sweltering in the heat of injustice and oppression, will be transformed into an oasis of freedom and justice.

I have a dream that my four children will one day live in a nation where they will not be judged by the color of their skin but by the content of their character.

I have a dream today ...

Sir Winston Churchill

Hitler knows he will have to break us on this island or lose the war. If we can stand up to him, all Europe may be free, and the life of the world may move forward into broad, sunlit uplands. But if we fail, the whole world, including the United States, including all we have known and cared for, will sink into the abyss of a new Dark Age made more sinister and perhaps more protracted by the lights of perverted science. Let us therefore brace ourselves to our duties and so bear ourselves that if the British Empire and its Commonwealth last for a thousand years, men will still say 'This was their finest hour.'

The first two of these statements of course involve companies that still exist. Neither of these companies have been without their problems and both face considerable competition that didn't exist when they were founded. But if the sincerest form of flattery is in imitation, then they can both be proud of the fact that others have sought to copy them.

Charles Handy gave the best definition of a vision I have come across when he wrote, 'A vision must be different. A vision has to reframe the known scene, reconceptualize the obvious and connect the previously unconnected dream.' All of the above visions were simple, they did reframe the known scene, they did reconceptualize the obvious and they did connect the previously unconnected dream.

And all of these visions have come to fruition. Charles Handy went on to say that a vision should create the 'ah' effect. When a person goes 'ah, I see what you mean' or 'ah, that feels good to me,' they have been able to see or grasp the concept and place it into perspective to where they are now.

I would bring your minds back to the definition of leadership that I used from Norman Schwarzkopf, that a leader is able to make people follow willingly. The ability of the leaders quoted above to get people to follow willingly rested with the passion with which they put over their vision and the depth of passion with which they pursued their vision.

So, as I outlined in the introduction to vision in the last

chapter, what is needed is 'Vision with Passion.' However, I would now like to qualify this requirement of a leader.

Yes, you need a vision and yes, you need to convey this with passion. This can be the thundering passion of Martin Luther King or the quiet passion of someone like Mother Theresa, but in every case there is something very distinctive about the way in which the vision is conveyed and which must be mastered.

There is a quote that says, "A leader is anyone who has two characteristics: first he is going somewhere; second, he is able to persuade other people to go with him." Going back to the analogy of driving the car, it is difficult to get people as passengers if there is no purpose to the drive. However, if you are going somewhere specific, it is easier to get passengers assuming that they also want to go to the same place. If there is more than one driver going to that place or you really want company and the potential passengers are not sure they want to go, then it becomes important that the driver "is able to persuade others to go with him."

It therefore becomes the leader's job to 'sell' the vision to the potential followers so that it makes absolute sense to them to follow. When we are selling a product we are exhorted to dwell on the benefits and not on the features.

If we look again at the vision statements of the great leaders above, we can see that they knew their audience and could sell the benefits of their vision in the same way. Henry Ford has targeted the ordinary man and dangles the benefit of enjoyment with his family in the open spaces of the country, and he also dangles the benefit of well-paid work to the masses. Walt Disney also offers the benefit of inspiring and motivating our children as well as providing wonderful entertainment for the whole family. Martin Luther King provides vivid images for the black people of America, making the benefits of freedom and justice come alive for all that hear him. Finally, Sir Winston Churchill also paints pictures of what life would be like on the one hand if everyone resisted Hitler, and on the other if they failed to overcome him. He offers the benefit of sunlight in their lives if they rise up and fight.

This gives us the three requirements of a leader contained in his or her EXTERNAL expression or communication process:

- to have a vision that people can buy into or be motivated by

- to articulate it in a way that is meaningful to the individual or group that receives it

- to help people be focused with a clear personal understanding of the future.

How good are you at these aspects of providing a VISION for your people or even for yourself?

Vision and mission

I mentioned already that there is a difference between a 'vision' and a 'mission' or 'purpose.' A mission is a statement of purpose. A mission outlines the purpose of the organization or why the organization is in existence. Another way of looking at it is to imagine what you want your company to mean to the man in the street. If you have a restaurant, you may want the man in the street to say, "Oh yes, that restaurant is the best Italian food restaurant in town and it is good value." In which case the mission may be "To provide the best Italian food in town with good value for money."

When it comes to the 'Vision,' a vision is an understanding or a visual representation of the future. So for the above example the vision may be expressed by the owner as "People will come here for a taste of Italy. To feel the atmosphere that can only be generated when good Italian wine and pasta come together, to eat the food 'Mama' would make ..."

The vision will bring the mission or purpose to life in a manner that captures the imagination of the people and helps them understand a little of what they are expected to do to achieve it. In some cases, the mission can be the vision. Normally these are cases when the purpose of the organization is not currently being met and so the mission or purpose of the organization becomes a vision in itself.

Charles Handy goes on to say: "A vision must be understandable. No one can communicate a vision that takes two pages to read, or is too full of numbers and jargon. It has to be a vision that sticks in the head. Metaphors can be the keys because they provide vivid images with room for interpretation, i.e. low definition concepts as opposed to the more precise high definition words of engineering and management. A vision remains a dream without the work of others. It has to be their vision too, and their ideas should be heeded."

Please note that a mission statement is not mandatory. Bear in mind that organizations like Marks and Spencer did not have a mission statement and equally there are a lot of poor performing organizations that have a mission statement that is just a group of words on a wall. However, the leader does need the ability to have a vision and then articulate that vision to people.

At this point, I want to make a point about the vision. The content does not necessarily have to be precise. It depends on who the vision is aimed at and the circumstances surrounding the organization. Obviously there is no need to give away secrets that could be commercially sensitive. There has to be enough information to give credibility to the vision and with enough information that people can believe that it is possible, but there is not a requirement to be overly specific.

Equally, the vision will not give extensive details about the 'how' it will be achieved. People, as we shall discuss later, need to be allowed to bring their own creativity and place themselves in the picture. Being prescriptive about the 'how' can make people feel excluded or stop them contributing to the full extent.

Developing the Vision

Senior executives often spend countless hours putting together a vision for their company. If you are in such a company, would you be able, right now, to tell the next person you meet exactly what your vision is? If you can't, then the chances are that the vision is not working for you. As a leader, you should be able to express yourself and not recite a prepared speech. Here are some helpful hints to test your vision:

There are certain requirements for a vision.

- A vision must take what people will probably already know and bring it to life for them.

- A vision can be like a dream that may, or may not, come true but is worth working towards.

- A vision must be understandable.

- A vision will require the work and commitment of others than yourself.

- A vision should be short and simple.

- A vision should be memorable.

- A vision should come from your heart.

Note that while I say that a vision should come from the heart,

I have not said that it is something that should be reproduced off by heart. The examples I have used are good examples of visions that had a conviction about them that was as important as the message.

A vision encompasses an overall picture of what it will be like. It is not just an intellectual understanding, but it moves into the emotional level by creating a feeling within people. To say "we are going to be the best at making widgets" is not nearly as powerful as "we are going to make the highest standard of widgets and set the standard in the industry for others to copy."

A leader understands the need to be able to present a vision in a manner that will fire the imagination of the people expected to make it happen. In some cases, it is to reconceptualize the already known. For example, "We will not only make the best widgets and be better than our competitors, but we will provide a 'Rolls Royce' service to go with the widget." This takes the present position of what we already do and moves the stakes up a little more so that it becomes a new motivating force.

What is really interesting though is the way the leader is able to adapt his vision. In the example above, the leader may come across a lorry driver who is feeling depressed with his job because he has just spent the last three hours stuck in a major traffic jam. Consoling the driver with the words "We will not only make the best widgets and be better than our competitors …" is not likely to lift the man's spirits. However, if the leader puts himself into the driver's shoes and says something like: "I know driving can be a tough job with today's traffic conditions. We've been making a lot of changes round here to improve the quality of our service and we're proud to have drivers as dedicated as you. And just imagine what it will be like when you pull into a service station and all the other drivers ask you if that's your vehicle. When you say 'yes,' they'll tell you how lucky you are and how they wish they were able to work with your company because of the reputation we have for first class quality and service."

The message however, would be different for the sales manager, who was perhaps feeling despondent because he had just lost a client to a competitor with a lower price. The leader would acknowledge that it's impossible sometimes to hang onto every client in an industry as competitive as the widget industry, but consoles him with: "… but don't worry. With the changes we have been making around here, our quality and service are going to be so good, that the client will sooner or later realize that price isn't everything and will come back to us."

A client in the contract cleaning business faced the problem of lacking a vision and we worked on it to create a new level of business for him, his staff and his customers. The vision was a move from being a contract cleaning company that cleaned up other people's mess, to a company that took care to ensure their client's image was always at the highest standard for their customers, and that their staff had a clean working environment at all times. This is reconceptualising what has already been done in a manner that can fire the imagination.

Tunnel Vision

It is worth noting that the leader has vision but this is not 'tunnel vision.' It does not mean that the leader gets locked into a particular direction and is so focused that he or she loses touch with opportunities or even, on occasions, alternatives. What is does mean is that the leader does not change track or move the direction on an ad-hoc basis. Leaders, as we shall see later, are good listeners and are always willing and receptive to new ideas. However, they are not prepared to be deviated from their course without just cause. If there is a good reason to change then it is considered and acted upon but it is not on a whim.

I have come to understand this more as time has passed. Because the leader has taken so much time to prepare the vision and instill it into people in a manner that captures their imagination, they can't afford to lose that strength they have harnessed without good reason.

Due to the nature of the world at the moment, most organizations are going through constant change. I often get asked how it is possible to set a vision when one doesn't know what will happen tomorrow?

In setting the vision, the leader warns people of the need to be responsive and adaptable to changes when they arise. "It doesn't matter what the market place does, we will always be responding to it faster than anyone else and we will remain flexible to adapt to those demands through our attitude and approach to doing business."

The leader has an intuitive understanding of the underlying factors that govern every person's behavior and so guides their emotion. The first of these is the need for certainty. People need to have a level of certainty and a vision helps go a long way towards achieving that. In the case where there is no certainty, because change is the norm, a leader will turn that around and make the uncertainty a certainty that they can make use of.

It's interesting how they arrive at the vision. Leaders are not always very creative and original thinkers. They are, however, good listeners and always ask and listen to the thoughts of people in the team, customers and even competitors. They piece together bits of what people say and get a fix on the direction through a great deal of research. They are searching for an angle which will give their organization an edge or an advantage or just set them as different from the run of the mill. They recognize that innovation is what will win the day whether that be in product or service, and they search for that.

As much as they are good listeners they also realize that the customer doesn't always know what he or she wants. If we only listened to the customer, progress would be slow. For example, nobody asked for the camcorder and yet it has been an outstanding success. The leader is not frightened to break new ground and walk the fine line between listening to the customer and being innovative. Akio Morita of Sony had a vision to bring 'personal portable sound to every man,' and so the hugely successful Sony Walkman was born.

Those that spend all their time listening and not making a move until everyone is happy, never make it to being a leader in the eyes of their people. It is the boldness to weigh up the facts, listen to the evidence and then make a decision that sets them apart. So when leaders consult and then make a decision, they ensure that they are able to set the direction in the form of a vision that will inspire and motivate people to make it happen.

SUMMARY

➤ A vision is different from a mission or purpose.

➤ A vision makes the mission or purpose come to life.

➤ A leader must be able to create a vision.

➤ A leader can articulate a vision.

➤ A vision comes from the heart of the leader.

➤ A vision will enable people to make a commitment.

6

Values as a Foundation to Leading

We have discussed how it is the 'Integrity' of the Leader in the eyes of the people that provides the basis for Leadership. Integrity is based on a person's set of values. So what are values?

The word 'value' is commonly used to describe what something is worth. Usually it is used in monetary terms but can also be used in terms of time spent or resources allocated. Marketing people use the term 'added value' to describe giving the perception of something being worth more or the worth being enhanced in some way.

However, the word 'values' (adding the 's') tends to be used in terms of people or organizations. For example, he or she 'has a good set of values' or, in a negative context, he or she 'has no values.' What do we mean? Surely we don't mean that they are worthless? It can't mean that they have no monetary value.

A dictionary might define values as, 'the social principles, goals or standards held by an individual, class, society, etc.' Here we see the use of the word 'principle.' The same dictionary might explain the word 'principle' as, 'a rule of conduct, adherence to such rules; integrity.' The word 'standard' is explained as 'something established as a rule... a usage or practice that is generally accepted.'

It would seem that the word 'values' refers to some form of

rule. Not just any rule, or rules, but ones that are accepted by the majority. Interestingly, we also see the word 'integrity' being used which the dictionary defines as 'honesty.' This implies that the rules should be within the bounds of integrity or honesty. This would explain why the word 'values' is used in the context of people and organizations.

So, 'values' means people or organizations that are recognized by others as having standards based on integrity and honesty. Equally those that have no values are being referred to as not having standards of integrity and honesty that are recognized by others.

How do we choose our values?

Values are not something that we can choose to have or not to have as the case may be. We all have values, including organizations. It is like breathing. We don't have a choice of whether we breathe or not, we have to breathe. The choice is in how we breathe to get the best for ourselves. The same choice applies to values. We can choose our values or we can allow our values to be formed for us by circumstances or other people. I call this forming values by design or by default.

It should be noted that before leaders can define the values of their organization, it is important they define their own personal values! Since values decide the way we behave and so subsequently the way we do business, to instill values, the senior management need to be able to 'walk the talk' or do it themselves first. Defining personal values then lays the foundation to build organizational values which in turn leads to improved levels of performance through new behavior patterns.

If you want to know what your current values probably are, then find out what people say about you behind your back!

All behavior patterns are based on values or rules. In other words the way someone behaves is based on his or her values. We all behave in accordance with the values we have developed within ourselves. So where do these values come from? Values, (principles or rules) have been based on beliefs. What we believe will or will not happen in any given circumstance decides our values. If we believe that dogs are dirty animals that spread disease, then we are likely to have values that decide that we should not come into contact with these animals or not let them into our house or not let children play with them, and so on. So the belief about dogs creates the behavior pattern.

Where do our beliefs come from? Beliefs are based on the interpretation we give to experiences we undergo. The belief that dogs are dirty and spread disease may be based on an experience either we had or someone we knew had with a dog that made either them or us ill.

Everything we do creates an experience from which we make a meaning and then, based on that meaning, we decide what are the rules or principles that we learn from it. The operative word is 'decide.' Once a decision is made, we have laid down some rules or principles (values) which we will then live by. Living by them means we will behave in accordance with those rules. Hence our behavior is generated by the principles we hold within ourselves.

To illustrate, let's say we work for someone who doesn't give praise or recognize our efforts. Our interpretation of this may be that this boss (or even bosses generally) don't care about people who work for them and they just take people for granted. Once we have adopted this interpretation, this then becomes a belief. We may even justify the belief by saying to ourselves that it is pointless to work hard because no matter what we do, it will be taken for granted. This belief generates us into a behavior pattern which may lead us to not bother and not put too much energy into what we do.

Our interpretation to every event, ultimately sets our values.

Those values then form the basis of our lives.

How do we know what our values are at present?

The simplest way to do this is to list out what is most important to you in your life and put it in priority order. It is vital that you are honest with yourself and, to do this, it will help if you can describe next to the list you have chosen what needs to happen for you to achieve these states. By describing what is important to you and then describing what has to be happening to achieve it, you have identified some of your values.

Now think about what qualities leaders need to have towards their people. List these out and be sure that there are none that are incompatible. If they are not compatible then you will need to change them.

(You may take the opportunity to do the same exercise relating to your position as a friend, partner, lover, family, etc.)

For example mine are:

To be calm, patient, honest, humble, focused, positive, adventurous and approachable, while having strength of character and belief in myself.

(For my relationships with my family, I add the words 'loving' and 'lovable' because they are important to me in a family context. On a personal level I also add the word 'healthy' because without good health, I will never achieve what I want and be what I need to be for others.)

These become your values in life and form the basis for your actions as a leader. Take this list and re-read the list of values and decide if there are any that should not be there or are in the wrong order for what you want to achieve. It would also be helpful to think about why these are important to you.

The big trick is to live by these values. The way you do this is to start reading these every day for at least three times a day.

If you ever act out of character with your code of conduct, then take time out to study the code, the values and the states which you need to achieve to maintain these values. Also re-read the reasons why you made the change and the consequences of not making the change.

As with any habit, it takes time to change but you will be amazed at how quickly you will move through this transformation. You will also be proud of yourself because the values will have been decided by you and not evolved out of your control.

What has this to do with companies or organizations?

Companies and organizations also have values. These are the operating standards by which they will carry out their business. *These values decide the behavior patterns in the organization in the same way that they do in people.*

For example, I recently had the pleasure to visit a nursing home for the elderly. The aim of this organization was 'to provide whole person care.' They described this as caring for the residents physically, mentally and spiritually. Staff were expected to treat the place as though they were in the home of one of the residents. The staff believed that it was not just a place to work but rather it was the home of the residents and they were treat it as if they were in their home. You can imagine the impact that these values had on the way the staff went about their daily duties.

I equally visited a dealership which required their staff to be polite to the customers and the company even tried to provide training in Customer Care. They tried hard to get the staff to understand that they should be taking an interest in the customers and that they should promote various products and services to them. However, when speaking to the senior management team, I discovered that they believed that the staff were employed to do the job they were told to do! Added to this, they believed that their customers were miserly and that selling was a 'game of chess' where there are winners and losers.

You can imagine the values that permeated through this company and the resulting actions by both staff and customers. The staff did what they had to do. They played it by the book, they treated the customers just right, they acted the part and at the same time believed that their employer was trying to con the customers and probably was doing the same to them. Their ability to provide genuine customer care was limited by the 'values' permeating through the company.

The importance of this for organizations who are competing in the modern world, starts to become more evident. We are living in days when the product does not provide the difference between us and our competitors.

 These days, the quality and price we offer only allows us access to the playing field.

Service is the cutting edge and service means people. If we want to get the most out of people then we need to make sure they have the same values that we have in our organization. These values need to line up and be in congruence. If the values are conflicting then we are wasting resources, time and money, and giving away the edge to our competitors.

The sad thing is that most organizations can't even define their values. They have been formed by chance and not through thought and forward thinking. However, the organizations that are making the biggest steps in performance and return on investment are clear about their values.

I recently found an organization that believes that its 'values' are the true chief executive of their business. They have defined their values so clearly that the values manage the business. In the case of the nursing home, the final decision maker is: what is in the best interests of the residents in their home?

Their values could be summed up as follows:

- Be ethical.

- Be responsive.

- Be profitable.

These three guiding principles (values) manage the business. The result is a satisfying place of work and an outstanding home for the residents and peace of mind for their families.

The values of the dealership could also be summed up as follows:

- Make money.

- Be nice.

- Behave.

These three guiding principles (values) manage their business as well. The result is that staff do not contribute to the business, they do what they have to do and customers shop there because they have little in the way of choice. This company does not, and will never, achieve maximum performance.

Values have a huge impact on the success of a business and it is the leader who should be defining the values. Not only do leaders define the values, they should be walking, talking, breathing examples of these values in action. They should personify the values they expect of others.

SUMMARY

➤ Values mean having standards of integrity and honesty that are recognized by others.

➤ If you want to know what your current values are, then find out how people talk about you behind your back.

➤ The beliefs we have are based on the interpretations we've made from the experiences we have had.

➤ Our beliefs form our values which govern our behavior.

7

Love of People

I am sometime challenged about the use of the word 'love' in relation to this section. It is not my intention to describe this in terms of the way we liberally use the word for a range of relationships. Rather the intention is to describe the mindset that the leader has with relation to people.

As we will discover in this chapter, the mindset of a leader has a big impact on the way a leader behaves as well as the way that important issues are dealt with.

A mindset about people

In simple terms the mindset is; 'people are important.' Not the 'most' important, not more important than any other aspect of running a successful organization and not less important than making a profit. The statement simply says that 'people are important.'

The best way it was explained to me was, if any organization was able to do all the jobs required to be done within it by one person, then there would only be one person in that business! Logical when you think about it. However, because there are so many duties to be carried out (marketing, sales, design, development, administration, accounts ...) different people are employed to carry out the various functions. If we follow the same thread of thought logically, then we must also deduce that the effectiveness of any organization will be the ability of all the individuals to be able to work together as though they were a single person.

Again we need to accept that, as pivotal as this will be, it is only one of many pivotal aspects of a successful organization. Others include the ability to identify the market trends, the ability to be innovative and so on. This is why I said that it is not the most important but that it is important.

So when we refer to 'people being important,' we are saying that they each have a role to play, and the way that they perform in that role has a direct impact on the performance of that organization. A leader understands this inherently.

The effects of this mindset

While visiting organizations, you can learn much about an organization by asking what the communication is like.

I have discovered that 'communication' is largely a perception issue! It is not really down to whether there is good communication within any organization, rather it is about whether it is perceived as good.

People use communication as an excuse when the situation is actually more fundamental than that. As a rule, nobody would admit out loud that their boss was awful or simply poor at being a boss. Equally they won't come out and say that the company is a terrible place to work. Even when they do admit it and you press for a reason to substantiate it, they will invariably say that the communication is poor.

The truth of the matter is, communication is a good (and easy) excuse for why people feel the wrongs of a company are happening. It is easy to say and hard to refute. Even in the best performing organizations, you will always find examples of where people do not get information.

To test the truth of the matter, you can go into two branches of the same organization, i.e. a supermarket, fast-food restaurant or tire fitters, which both have the same systems for passing on information. They will have all the normal methods including notice boards, memos, emails, team meetings, early-morning briefings, etc. However, visit one and ask the people who work there what it is like as a place to work. They will say that it is great. They will say that it is friendly, people are good to talk to and supportive, and when you ask about communication, they will say that they get to know everything that is going on.

You go into the other and ask the same questions and they will say that the place is 'alright' or 'okay' expressed in a non-committal way. When you push, they will invariably say that 'you never know what is going on' or 'you are generally kept in the dark.' Now, the question I ask is this: why when both places have the same systems in place and both groups are receiving the same information at the same time, does one feel that they don't know and the other feel that they get to know everything?

This is why I believe that 'communication' is a perception issue. It is not whether the people know everything or not, it is whether they believe that they are being kept informed. In branch A, I can point out that they weren't told something and they will respond with something like "Well everyone makes mistakes." In branch B, I can point out that they weren't told something and they will say "You see, that's what I mean, we don't get told what is going on around here." If you perceive that you are well-informed, then you will excuse the times when you don't get to hear as 'human error' or 'we all make mistakes.' However if you perceive that communication is poor, then you will seize any examples as evidence that you are right.

Let's go back to branch A and branch B. What is the difference between them? If they both have the same systems in place and are using them, why do the people in one respond so negatively and the other respond so positively?

The major difference between the two are the people who lead the two branches. As I said already, the communication is used as a safe excuse to blame the ills of the company or branch or department. The real reason is the poor leadership in the area of this element, 'Love of People.'

Leaders who are good at this element are not always the best communicators! However, they are very good at providing the perception that everything is okay and their people know everything. People pick up on this mindset and perceive that their leader will ensure that they are told everything they need to know, and more beside if necessary. They perceive the leader as approachable and if they want to find something out they perceive that individual as caring about their role in this organization.

What do leaders do that creates this appearance or perception?

They create the environment where people believe that they know what they need to know and have faith in the leader that he or she will keep them informed. A lot of this has to do with having the integrity that we talked about in the previous chapter.

In the case of communication, their mindset was firstly that communication is important and that it needs to be two-way. Secondly, that the communication must be about things that people want to know about and not what management think they should know.

1. Important and two-way
I recently visited an organization that was very proud of the systems in place for communication. They had notice boards

that were full of information and copies of minutes from meetings. They had flow charts and performance figures showing progress everywhere. They had weekly team-briefings and handover meetings for those that worked in the factory and did shift work. As far as having systems for communication in place, they were an excellent example and they had their hands on the wheel in the way they had been taught at driving school.

However, when I spoke to the staff, one of the biggest complaints was the lack of communication! So I pursued it in hope of finding the real problem. The answer was easy to find really. They said that managers in the business didn't listen to any ideas that people were giving. They did not feel that the management was listening or even wanted to know what they had to say.

People had ideas to help improve the business, but they felt nobody wanted to know. They had suggestions, but they had given them in the past and nothing had been done about it. The funniest (or saddest) part of this story was that the management told me two things. They said the staff 'aren't interested'! Then they went on to say that nobody talks at the team meetings other than the occasional question for clarification!

If it wasn't so serious it would be hilarious. On the one side we have the staff saying that the managers don't listen and are poor communicators and on the other side we have the managers saying that the staff are not communicative and aren't interested anyway.

Good leaders know that communication is a two-way process. It requires getting the message across as well as making sure you receive information by listening. My grandmother told me that I had two ears and one mouth and I should use them in that proportion because God had given me them to be used in equal balance. I didn't appreciate the value of those words of wisdom until later in life and I will endeavor to explain why in the next chapter.

2. Communication needs to be relevant

In this same organization I discovered that, despite all the systems in place, the communication was not only a top-down communication system but also it was wholly lacking in crossways communication. For example, a hugely important order needed processing the week I was there – an important customer and a high priority. They knew the work was due and it had been planned for this week. No sooner had they started production, than maintenance needed to shut some of the production down to do work on the ceiling above which was absolutely necessary and had been planned for three weeks! Subcontractors were arriving, hire equipment was being delivered and men were ready to start work.

Nobody from maintenance had spoken to production and so the result was arguments, time and money wasted and staff saying "You see! Nobody knows what is going on around here."

Leaders are constantly aware of the impact of actions and the need to communicate the information as quickly and succinctly as possible.

Listening

Listening is a skill. Receiving the sound on the ear drum and making sense of it, is not a skill. That is physical and not related to listening. A similar example is tasting food. The process of receiving the food into the mouth, chewing on it and then swallowing it, is not tasting. The taste comes from the *interpretation* you give to the whole experience.

Before the food arrives in the mouth the senses of smell will have started to make some interpretations. Add then the sight of the food and then the environment you are in when you eat it, and you have and you have further interpretations before the food arrives in the mouth. Once in the mouth, you then combine the texture, strength and the ability to be broken down with your expectations and previous experiences and the taste is beginning to form in your mind. Your brain starts to make decisions about the taste and whether it is something that you like or don't like.

Listening goes through a similar process. As with the taste analogy, there are a lot of environmental issues that have a bearing on the mind's ability to listen. The frame of mind you are in when having the conversation will influence your ability to concentrate. The person and your perception of them will influence you and effect your interpretation of what they may be saying. If we then add the environment you are in when the conversation is taking place, the people present and the volume of background noise and so on, you can already see that the listening process is subject to a range of circumstances surrounding the sound arriving in the ear.

Somebody once said to me, "Isn't science wonderful? We can take a message and transmit it thousands of miles in split seconds." He then paused and added, "I wonder when we will manage the last few inches?"

The reason I say that listening is a skill is because it requires an effort and needs to be learned. I believe that taste is mostly learned in the same way as many other things we take for granted are learned. We learn to like or dislike various foods based on the experience we associate with the eating of it. To use a different example, I learned to smoke as a teenager. It was an awful experience but I decided that I needed to do this 'because grownup people smoke!' Having the second was not as bad as the first, the third not as bad as the second and so on. Eventually, I learned to enjoy the feeling and got hooked on the effects for many years. I do not smoke now, but what I find interesting is that I have not met anyone who found the experience enjoyable at the beginning. Yet they persisted until they found the enjoyment.

The same applies to taste. There are foods that I hated as a child that I have learned to like and in fact are now among my favorite foods. When I first tasted them, due to the environment or whatever, I hated the food and didn't want it. When faced with eating it, the memories would flood back of the first experience and I would relive that event all over again.

Listening is a similar process. When faced with a person who always complains about every little thing and they say, 'Can I have a word please?', what goes through your mind? How receptive are you to that person? Now add that you are in a hurry for an important meeting, how receptive are you? Now add that you catch sight of the person you are meant to be meeting and they are looking at their watch, how good are you at listening? Compare that situation with being all on your own with time to kill and being fully relaxed and at peace with your environment and the same person walks in and says 'Can I have a word please?'

I am sure you recognize that your ability to listen will be limited or you may feel it will be impossible in the first situation as compared to the second. Good leaders who have the ability to create the perception of being good communicators are able to deal with both situations, leaving the person feeling comfortable with the outcome.

 The leader will be focused on how that person perceives them and not on how they feel about that person or this situation.

The 'love of people' ability is not self-centered but rather based on recognizing that the person is important and so what they are saying is important *to them* even if the leader does not feel it is important at that moment. The leader will respond to the person by not letting personal beliefs, interpretations or feelings (self-centered) limit the ability to captivate this person and create the impression of being a good communicator.

Developing the skill of listening

I will endeavor to give you some simple tips that I have learned from watching those who are good at being listeners as well as talking to people who work for people who are good listeners.

The first step we will cover in the next chapter in more detail. The essence of it is, have the desire to be a good listener. The tips will then be a lot easier to develop. A lot of the ability will come from your frame of mind. My favorite is to tell yourself that what this person is telling you is the most important thing in the world to them at that moment. So important that they want to talk to you about it. The emphasis is on 'you' because they may have had other people they could go to or they may have had to overcome a range of self-doubts or lack of confidence to get the courage to speak to you about it.

Another comment worth saying to yourself is, I always tell people to come to me if they have a problem, issue or something they want support with. Now they have taken me up on that, the least I can do is to hear them out. Anything that you tell yourself that puts the situation into a context where you see the situation from their point of view without bias or prejudice will help adjust your frame of mind.

One person told me they forced themselves to remember times when they had gone to someone and had not been listened to. They reminded themselves of how that felt and that got them to realize the importance and prepared their mind to deal with the person.

The next tip I gleaned from them was the need to have a focus. Where we look when they are speaking sends out all sorts of signals about whether we are listening or not. Look at them in the eyes or at their face. Listen to the words and stop yourself formulating your conclusions prior to hearing theirs.

Remember, the human brain works at around 700 words a minute and that people speaking will speak at between 200 and 350 words a minute. So your brain is working faster than they can speak. It is natural for the brain to shoot off ahead and try to anticipate what the person will say. The skill a leader has is to limit that from making assumptions and cutting in before the person has finished. Let them say what they want and then respond taking into account what they have said and the way they have said it.

Repeating a persons words is a good way of showing you have listened.

Dealing with people

A wise person once said, "When rejecting the ideas of another, make sure you reject only the idea and not the person." Wise words indeed.

When we deal with people, we are dealing with living, breathing individuals who are a complex assortment of emotions and feelings as well as beliefs and prejudices. The ability to demonstrate the quality required in 'love of people' will require the leader to recognize this and act accordingly.

At this juncture I want to make something clear. 'Love of people' is not meant to mean that the leader must be a touchy-feely person full of care and consideration. There is nothing wrong with being a touchy-feely person, but leaders must also have their hard, practical side. In fact, I would say that being hard is one of the important aspects of being effective as a leader. The secret is knowing when and how to balance the two sides.

Stephen Covey described this very well when he refers to people's emotional bank account. In the same way that you would not draw out more from the bank than you deposit if you don't want to be overdrawn and have problems, a leader will not draw out of people's emotional bank account more than they personally put in.

You put into an emotional bank account in a number of ways. Listening is one, as are recognizing effort, greeting people when you see them, thanking them when they have made an effort, thanking them anyway, telling them things that interest them, showing an interest in what they do and all the other things we do to let people know we have noticed them and appreciate them.

Withdrawing from an emotional bank account is when we need to tell them something that will upset them or that has the possibility of affecting their confidence. Maybe they did something wrong, made a mistake, went about something in the wrong way, chose the wrong moment to deal with an issue or in someway did something that you need to point out to them.

SUMMARY

➤ Love of people is a mindset.

➤ The mindset of a leader is that "people matter."

➤ Communication is a perception issue.

➤ Listening is a habit that a leader has acquired.

➤ Leaders differentiate issues from personalities.

8

Nurturing Champions

Building on the mindset that a leader has about people in the previous chapter, we now move onto a quality which I describe as the 'most important' of all the qualities. I referred to the 'Consistent set of values' as the most powerful but this one is the most important and is fundamental to being a leader.

In all my research and all the interviews I held, I found that there is this fundamental attitude and quality in a leader. In simple terms, it is the willingness and desire to learn. Leaders are always seeking to develop themselves, expand their understanding, are keen to learn and have a desire to discover something new. This is not a pompous desire to know something that everyone else doesn't know but rather an inquisitiveness that allows them to get a wider perception of the world.

If you take the time to notice, one of the first things that strikes you about a leader is the number of questions they ask. Some people find this quite daunting and oppressive when they first come across what can appear as a barrage of questions. It is not meant to be aggressive but rather it is the leader's wish to achieve a greater understanding. Leaders will invariably take notes all the time because they don't want to miss anything, especially an idea that may be useful later. As Richard Branson said in an interview once, 'you will never remember all the things that are said to you' and a leader wants to capture everything to be used at the appropriate time.

In addition to having a personal insatiable desire to learn, a leader also encourages it in others. A leader will expect his or her people to have a similar desire and willingness to learn. Towards this end they will actively encourage any opportunity to expand knowledge in both themselves and for their people.

Nobody likes a smartass!

Think about it and it is obvious – who would you like to work for? Would you like somebody who always knew it all (even when they didn't) and was fearful of anybody knowing more than them, or would you prefer a person who was open to ideas, encouraged discussion and was always willing to listen and learn from anybody?

We have all come across the know-it-all who has done it all before and knows it all already. Even when they don't know anything about the subject they have to make comments to make themselves appear knowledgeable to the company they are in. These same individuals tend to talk louder as though this will increase your understanding of what they are trying to say. My observations have led me to believe that these individuals are actually insecure and conduct themselves in this manner as a way of overcoming their lack of confidence. It is exactly that point which limits them from becoming a leader in the eyes of their people. People aren't going to get confidence from someone who does not have confidence in themselves.

On the other hand we know how good it feels to be with someone who has confidence to the level where they aren't feeling threatened by other people's knowledge. They aren't intimidated by someone knowing more than they do – in fact, they encourage it. Their own confidence is not that fragile that they concern themselves with how clever you think they are. In fact, they expect that you will know more than them on some issues and are willing to learn from you in any area that you can offer valuable input.

The truth of the matter is, people like people who are smart but they don't like to feel intimidated by it or threatened in some way. The smart person doesn't do that, the smartass does.

There are also practical reasons why this is important and why I say that this is fundamental to being a leader.

The speed of change

We are living in a world where the pace of change is dramatic and there is no option but to stay with it. I am writing this on a computer that I bought three months ago and is already well out of date. I was speaking to someone yesterday who was describing voice recognition email. You can phone your computer from your mobile phone and have the computer read you your emails. This rush of change does not only apply to technology – the demands for customer service are greater than they were two years ago. Recently, I was in a hotel bar, and the poor service from the hotel was an open discussion among complete strangers waiting to be served. What would have been acceptable service two years ago is not now acceptable.

Look at the British icons of business like Marks and Spencer's, British Telecom and NatWest Bank who ten years ago led the field and now struggle to exist or have been taken over. This is change at a pace and size that we have not experienced before in the history of mankind.

Change means we need to adapt. Adapting means we need to be aware of what is happening and the possibilities that we have. Being aware means that we researching and seeking the information and weighing up the alternatives. Seeking information is learning in its simplest form. Leaders recognize this and adopt this attitude as a basis to being a leader.

However, there is more than just having the desire to gain information. Nurturing Champions is not about being inquisitive, it is about how you encapsulate the information and put it to best use or make it work for you. This requires the added features which a leader appreciates and makes use of.

Thinking

I mentioned above that a leader will "expect that you will know more than them on some issues and are willing to learn from you in any area that you can offer valuable input." The reason a leader is willing to listen to other people in this manner is a very simple concept but useful. It can be summed up in the old expression 'two heads are better than one.'

Our life is made up of a range of experiences and events that formulate beliefs and impressions about the world. Our interpretations are all different and we form the beliefs we have based on the interpretations we made at the time. So, the more experiences we bring to bear on the subject and the more we make use of the various interpretations people have made, the more we can discover and learn. Provided we are all seeking to achieve the same end and work within the same values, we have nothing to fear from allowing everyone to contribute their ideas. No one person will have all the answers because no one person has all the knowledge in the universe and, even if they did, they have not had all the possible experiences and interpretations to add to the knowledge.

So "two heads are better than one" is more than two lots of knowledge. It is two lots of experiences, two lots of perceptions, two lots of interpretations and two lots of understandings. If we then add to this, as each thought is generated in one brain, it immediately challenges the other brain and unlocks new perceptions, interpretations and understandings, thus creating a compounding effect. So two brains don't generate double the number of ideas. Two brains will produce as many more ideas as there are perceptions, understandings and interpretations.

There is nothing to fear from this. It does not make one person better than the other but rather it potentially makes the two more powerful. The factors that contribute to making this a success are:

- both parties being willing to contribute.

- both parties being willing to accept ideas.

- both parties respecting the other's interpretations, experiences and perceptions.

The level to which the ideas can be generated based on the above will now be regulated by the breadth of experiences that the parties both have. What is interesting about this is that intelligence is not the biggest factor in contributing to the ideas.

I am always reminded of the story of the lorry that got stuck under the bridge. A child walked by and asked what had happened? The police explained that they were trying to find how to get the truck out from under the bridge. They had engineers, mechanics and a range of specialists looking at the situation. The child tried to speak again and was told to stay out the way. He watched in fascination as these clever minds argued about the possibilities and when he tried to push his way forward to speak he was told to get out the way. Finally, the men stopped talking long enough for the young boy to shout at them, "Why don't you just take some air out of the tires?!"

The boy was not intellectually brighter than the group of

engineers, mechanics, builders and others. However, he did have a perspective that none of the others had. It was not until they were at the point where they were willing to listen and learn that they were able to grasp the obvious and see the way to move out of the problem by listening to the child.

When someone has the characteristics of 'Nurturing Champions' they:

- constantly tune their mind into the possibilities to learn from any source that can add value irrespective of where it comes from

- are aware and respect that there will be different experiences, interpretations and understandings in each person.

Finally, there is one last element to *being a leader* that needs to be understood to make this work. A leader does not jump to conclusions or make assumptions.

Isn't it true that those who know it all are also the same people who don't let you finish speaking before they have jumped in and started to reply to what you are saying? You can see those that try to control it but you can tell that they have stopped listening and are just waiting for you to stop speaking so they can tell you the answer to what they think you are saying.

Being a leader is listening to what is being said and not to what you think is being said. I mentioned a while ago that the rate we speak and the rate we can think has a variance of anything from 250 to 450 words a minute. This is why we have a tendency to take the essence of what is being said and formulate our thoughts and plan our reply. This is called making an assumption. However, while we are doing this we are no longer listening and we are not hearing what the person is actually saying.

Assumptions are dangerous because they demonstrate lack of self-control, lack of patience, lack of respect and a closed mind. None of these characteristics are what a person is looking for in a leader and do not encourage respect or build integrity.

Developing a learning mind

In the last chapter and this one, I explained the mindset of leaders in the area of dealing with people as well as their attitude to learning. I want to spend a bit of time giving you the practical tips I have discovered on how a leader seems to achieve this mindset.

'Listening' has come up as an important aspect of showing people that you care as well as being necessary for the ability to learn. There is another dimension that compliments listening and is even more powerful in its ability to improve people's performance.

The secret is the ability to ask questions. Just listening is not always going to be helpful. When we are listening, the other person is controlling the conversation and telling us what they want us to hear. It is like being at a concert. We go because we want to hear a specific type of music or a particular person singing. After that, we are not in control of how they deliver it to us and we receive what they give. When we are just listening, we may have control in choosing who we are conversing with, but when we sit back and let them speak, we are not in control of the conversation or the direction it takes.

What allows us to contribute in a constructive manner as well as cover all the aspects we have gone into in this chapter is the ability to ask good questions. Also, questions are very powerful to ensure that the conversation stays on track and moves forward progressively.

As passive listeners, we are taking in information, most of

which we will forget within a couple of days, whereas the person asking questions is seeking to understand or to find a practical application for the knowledge he or she is receiving. The questions are a vehicle for extracting the information and enough of the information to ensure that action can be taken.

Asking questions also:

- sends the person a signal that you have been listening

- shows that you are still listening and are interested

- helps keep you focused, because if you are thinking about the next question instead of your reply, then you are still listening

- opens the other person's mind further and lets you gain additional information he or she may not have told you yet

- seeks clarification and stops your jumping to conclusions or making assumptions.

All of these are very powerful in terms of *being a leader*. It is also highly practical if we take some time to understand the brain and how it works.

The Brain

The brain is the most complex piece of equipment known to man. It is beyond the ability of man to replicate it because of its complexity. On the one side, it records data and information but at the same time it also attaches interpretations to certain information it receives. For example, one and one is two. This is factual data and it is easily stored and retrieved as necessary. Hair on a man's chin is a beard. Again factual data, but in this case I can also attach a belief about this. For example, I can believe that men with beards are unkind. This may be because I had a bad experience with a bearded man when I was a child. Whatever my reason, the belief attached to that is personal and will affect my behavior.

This ability to take knowledge and attach emotions to it is what makes the brain so unique but also so complex. However, it does not end there. The brain is also in control of deciding what information is relevant to us based on the experiences we accumulate and the interpretations we give them. Go back to the examples of the bearded man. Based on my belief, what am I going to notice about men with beards? I will tend to notice anything that proves my opinion and substantiates my belief. Even when I meet a man with a beard who is very kind and nice, I excuse this as the exception rather than change my opinion.

If we can appreciate how this works, then let us go back to the power of asking questions. What does a question do? As far as thinking is concerned, a question can accomplish one of two things depending on where it is asked and the way it is asked.

- A question asks for information.

- A question challenges the information it is receiving

Both are very useful. One question is 'What are we doing?' and the other is 'Why are we doing it like that?'

What is really fascinating about all this is that the brain is working at its best when it is being questioned. Think about how you talk to yourself. We all talk to ourselves and that is quite normal. However, notice how much of the conversation is in terms of questions.

- Where did I put my keys?

- What shall I do now?

- What is that idiot doing?

- I wonder what is happening ...?

- I wonder what we shall have for supper tonight?

- When is the car due for a service?

A great deal of out internal dialogue is in terms of questions. We are asking the stored data and the emotions we have to give us meaning to what we see or the situation we are in. Based on this, we take the relevant action.

What makes this so interesting is the power of asking the questions. Not just any question but the 'right' question. My research showed that the good leaders were good at asking questions. They were probing and trying to learn and understand so that they could develop themselves and their organization. They seem to realize the value of knowledge and acquiring knowledge and endeavored to use their brain in a way that increased its potential.

They also aimed to help people do the same for themselves. It was not uncommon to find that a leader would get two people together to 'see what would happen.' The leader seems to instinctively know that people coming together in the right environment could achieve great things. One of the fundamentals of that environment is the willingness to learn.

SUMMARY

➢ A leader is willing to learn.

➢ A leader encourages others to learn.

➢ Leaders makes the best use of the brain capacity of all those around them.

➢ A leader uses questioning as a means of unleashing the capability of the brain.

9

Overview – the Final Frontier

This trait is the hardest for most to achieve and maintain. It requires a strength from within, and this strength does not come easily to most people. It requires maintaining a balance which is at best precarious and at worst fatal in ensuring a successful relationship between the leader and his or her followers.

Overview is a combination of delegation and empowerment with a whole lot of trust included at the same time. Tom Peters described it as, "training the hell out of people and then getting out of their way and allowing the them to get on with the job they are paid for." In the last section, we discussed the importance of training and developing people. This section is all about the "getting out of their way and allowing them to get on with it."

My research showed something that is really interesting. When I talked to leaders, many thought that they weren't very good at delegating and empowering. They actually said that it was something they constantly struggled with. Then I went and talked to their staff, who said they were really brilliant at it. That made me inquisitive. Why? What's going on? And the reason I found was simply this. A leader sees people as individuals and is constantly working with these individuals on a one-to-one basis when delegating and empowering them. One of the basic concepts that leaders seem to have grasped is "don't treat everyone the same."

Sounds simple, but in reality it is one of the hardest things that people in a position of authority have to do. It is hard for the most experienced person, never mind the would-be leader trying to develop these skills in the world today. It requires the same discipline that a parent needs when their child starts to grow up and venture out into the world. It is so easy to tell them what to do for fear they will make the same mistakes we once made. However good the intentions are, parents ends up creating animosity between themselves and their children if they don't let go and allow them to figure things out for themselves. We all know this because we have all been there!

The danger is that some people recognize the need to stand back and let people get on with it, but still have a problem with the concept and so they walk away totally. It is the difference between 'delegation' and 'abdication.' While walking away is an easy way to come to terms with the situation because it relieves the pain of watching them make what to us are the most obvious mistakes, it is in reality the worst thing to do. A balance is required between the need to 'let go' and allow people the opportunity to do things on their own, and the opposite which is to 'abandon' them to their own devices.

Teaching a child to swim is a good illustration. During training, we would remain in the water, working with the child, to develop the stroke and momentum to be able to swim. Finally the child starts to move without our support. At this stage, we wouldn't get out of the pool and head off home. No, we would stay in the pool and give the child some advice, watching over the learning swimmer for a while. When we were more confident, we would then get out and sit close at hand so that we were there if we were needed. Only when both parties were confident, would we be comfortable to allow the child to go swimming on his or her own.

Delegation and empowerment requires the same process. First there is the training and development to a level of competency where individuals can manage on their own. Then we move to the hands-off stage (not the run off stage). As confidence grows, so the distance between you grows so that you can eventually leave them to manage the whole process without you.

Part of this process is allowing them to make mistakes. There is no point believing that we can point out all the disasters and provide a situation where they will not make any mistakes. Most things we need to learn require us to try them out and learn from the mistakes. In the same way, when we learned to swim, it didn't matter how many times we were shown or told how to do it, we only succeeded when we made the decision to have a go ourselves. When we did have a go, we didn't succeed first time. We tried and probably swallowed more water than we wanted to do. We tried again and then finally achieved the ability to remain afloat of our own accord. Even then, we sometimes got too confident and needed a sharp reminder of what was possible.

The same applies, to a greater or lesser extent, with anything we start for the first time whether it is riding a bicycle, speaking in public, working a piece of machinery or even getting on with people. A leader understands this and does not try to short-circuit it. The leader understands that time spent at this stage is well spent and that rewards will be reaped at the later stages.

Learning to let go

Maintaining the balance between not wanting to let go on the one hand, and on the other, letting go to the extent of abandoning them, is made all the more difficult by other weaknesses which are common to many people. The first is, as people successfully delegate and move on themselves to other things, they tend to lose touch with what happens now they are no longer involved closely with the function they delegated. We are aware of how times change and it is very easy to imagine that the job is as easy or straight forward as it was when we were doing it prior to delegation. This is not always true. In fact the probability is that it has changed and we may have to re-learn the requirements ourselves.

The second common failure is similar but in many ways worse. As people progress, they start to feel that they are above doing certain things. If a leader is viewed as being above doing certain jobs or functions they lose the humility which people warm to in a leader. People expect the strength of character, as well as humility of spirit from their leader.

It is for this reason I called this last section "Overview with overalls." The leader's willingness and desire to put on the overalls and help out at whatever level is necessary to support the team, is important.

It was put to me by one person that leaders 'work their butt off' planning and training their people and ensuring that they know what is expected of them. Then they sit back and are prepared to catch any aspect that falls down. This may be an over simplification but the essence is not far off. In reality, the leader is always busy because the business always needs reviewing and the plan needs modifying as progress is made. But the principle of setting people up to do what is required and leaving themselves as free as possible to respond to problems as they arise, is very sound. In other words, a leader plans then supports those that do it. Support cannot be limited to certain things that they like doing – it has to be whatever support is needed for the benefit of the whole.

Empowerment and delegation is the art of knowing when to let go, how much to let go and then how quickly to move away when you have let go. That is the balance that we are constantly trying to strike. It is a three-step process if you think about it. To delegate and empower somebody you need to think:

- how quickly you're going to let go of them

- how much do you let go, and

- once you've let go, how quickly or

how far do you step back?

At all times treating each individual individually remembering that no two individuals are the same. That is how delegation and empowerment is done.

The structure that enables the leader to let go

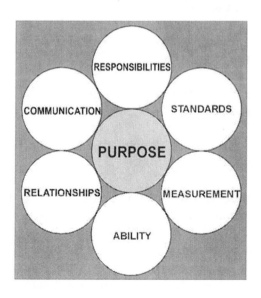

Figure 3 – Business structure

things like trust, training and communication are important but what makes these things hang together so that people can be empowered?

The whole structure hangs around the 'purpose' of the organization as you will see in figure 3.

- The purpose gives the reason for existence.

- To achieve the purpose, responsibilities are taken for various functions that together achieve the purpose.

- Standards are in place that ensure the purpose is achieved consistently as well as legally, safely and to a level of quality required.

- Measurement is in place that helps people know how they are progressing.

- Skills and knowledge are provided to achieve the purpose.

- Relationships are defined that describe the culture or ethos of the business.

- Communication allows and encourages participation and innovation to flourish.

This simple structure is understood at every level of the business. It is the reason you can buy a Big Mac in New York, London or Singapore and it will still be the same. It creates an environment where empowerment can thrive and people can take ownership for their role.

The key is the ability for everyone to understand their role in the process and how their role impacts on other people. For example, if a person in one area of responsibility is achieving the role perfectly towards the 'purpose' but in the process is hindering another person from being able to complete his or her role towards the 'purpose,' then the first person is failing! Simply doing your job well is not enough if it stops other people from achieving theirs.

Another important aspect is the distinctions between the 'purpose' and the 'standards.' In many organizations I visit, the standards are the purpose. Standards are a way to ensure the purpose is achieved consistently, safely and legally. It is not the reason for existence. People need to recognize this and remain focused on the purpose.

Measurement is important – but not for the reason a lot of managers think. Many managers introduce measurements as a way of policing people or checking up on them. This switches people's focus away from achieving the purpose to finding a way around the measurements. In truth, we all want measurements! It is human nature to want to know how we are doing. We want to know that the extra effort we put in achieved a result. However, the measurement needs to be relevant and not a threat. It needs to be constructive and fair, it needs to help us, not hinder us.

Providing the framework or structure that allows empowerment is a major benefit to creating an environment where people can be delegated to and will accept the power given to them.

SUMMARY

➤ A leader constantly works at the skills of empowering and delegating.

➤ A leader views people as individuals when delegating and handles each person differently.

➤ A leader provides the structure for empowerment to work..

➤ People at all levels understand the structure and their contributions within it.

$\overline{\underline{10}}$

Questions to Check Yourself Against the Attributes of a Leader

Vision

? **Are you clear about the long-term aims of the business/ team/group/organization?**

Many people say to me, "how can you be sure about the long-term aims of the business when the world is changing all the time? It is true that the world is changing all the time – no more so than presently, when terrorism and the threat of global conflict is so dramatic a factor in the development and success of major industries and companies. This question does not demand that you know exactly every detail but rather that you have some element of focus that gives you direction – something that you are aiming for or a purpose that is meaningful. It may be market share or possibly a size of operation or it may be down to positioning.

? Can you explain to people who work under your leadership what it will be like when you achieve your aims or vision?

Being able to articulate yourself is a skill that is very valuable for a leader. It is not about being able to explain your vision in a selfish way that makes it obvious that you will do well out of it. It is about being able to express your vision so that it captures *their* imagination. It is about being able to equate it to them in a manner that enthralls them, makes it seem worth while or gives them some pride to be associated with.

One of the great ways of achieving this is to get your people to be able to articulate it themselves. Help them be able to explain it to their people or their friends, family or customers. When they can describe it with passion, they will have really bought into it and made it their own.

? Do you take time to consider the various options for the future of your team, groups, business or organization?

How good are you at being able to step back from the situation and see if the way you are going is the best way of achieving your goals? It is very easy to get bogged down in the detail and forget the overall aim. We set out with a direction in mind and decide how we are going to get there. We then set about taking this route but we tend to try and "carry out the route" rather than get to the destination.

It is like taking the family out for the day and deciding to go to the seaside. We know what we want to do and we decide how we are going to get there. We set off and then run into a traffic jam. We sometimes get so focused on getting through the traffic and down to the sea that we forget what we set out to do. We wanted to have a day with the family by the sea. At any time, we could have possibly changed the route we had decided but we could equally have changed the destination to a different resort. Taking a step back may have also given us the option of going up the mountain because the real aim of the day was to spend a day with the family, enjoying each other's company.

? How good are you at moving away from the day-to-day activities and considering the implication for the future?

Similar to the above, this requires being able to look at things in a different light. Somebody once said to me, "many times, problems are nature's way of saying that we are going in the wrong direction." When issues arise, it may be that there are hidden opportunities in the issues. Some of the greatest inventions were the product of a mistake being made or a problem that turned out to be an opportunity.

The 'Post-it' note is an example. They were trying to make the best glue that had ever been made. One of the experiments produced a glue that didn't stick. Without the ability to step back and consider the implications for the future, that glue would have been assigned to the bin as a failure. Someone thought through the situation, found a use for it and as a result of that we have the post-it note and a massive industry was developed as a result.

I was once told the following story – I am not sure if it is true or not but it still makes the point.

A company making matches in the days when matches were in little boxes with sandpaper down the sides of the box had an employee who said he could save the company a lot of money. He asked if he could have 10% of the saving he would be making the company. The company refused, and the R & D department was given the task of finding the savings. After a while, when nobody could discover how to make such a huge saving, the board of directors agreed to pay the sum requested. The answer was simple, put sandpaper (used for striking the match) down one side of the box only and cut in half the amount of sand and glue being used.

The ability to step back and not allow yourself to get so close to the situation that you miss the opportunities or lose the chance to be substantially better than you realized is very useful when being a leader.

? Do you challenge the 'norm' as a way of clarifying the future?

Once again, similar to the above but this is not reacting to situations but rather actively challenging what is working very well. When the Royal Bank of Scotland (one of the smallest banks in Britain) took over the largest bank in Britain, NatWest, it was interesting how set in their ways NatWest had become. This large bank had become fixed in the way it was going about its business. I was told about one process or procedure having over twenty checks in place compared to the Royal Bank's three checks. When asked why there was so many checks the answer was "because that is always the way we have done it."

I am not doubting that each check was put into place for a valid reason at the time it was introduced. However, as procedures change, systems are developed or requirements change – nobody had asked "why are we still doing this check?"

Challenging the norm can achieve two things. It checks that what we are doing is still valid or necessary as in the above example. It also checks that we have thought it through completely. It reminds me of the story of the man who took his boss a proposal and his boss gave it back to him with the note saying "not good enough." He took it back and worked on it making it even better and including aspects in more detail and then re-submitted it. Once again his boss sent it back and "not good enough." This time the man really put his heart and soul into it. He thought about it again and put every possibility into the proposal. He was desperate and took the proposal into the boss personally and said, "I have done everything I can with this proposal, I have thought of every possibility and I have laid out every alternative available to us. If this is not acceptable, then I don't know what will be."

The boss replied, "Oh good. Now I'll read it!"

At first, this may sound heartless and I must agree I may not have taken that exact route to achieving the objective. However, the boss had got the person to think it though and challenge every possibility. By the way, the proposal was accepted.

Values

? Are you clear about what you stand for?

What are your values? You may say "Honesty is important to me." Well, if you do, then that is a good value. But let me ask you some questions.

- *When you are late for an appointment because you left too late, do you tell the truth as to why you are late or do you make an excuse?*

- *When you have made a mistake, do you always admit to it when asked or do you try to defend it in some way?*

Let's try another. The other one I am often asked is, "Being a law-abiding citizen is an important value." So let us try these questions:

- *Do you always keep to the speed limit?*

- *When the light changes from green to yellow, do you slow down to stop or race through?*

The answers to these questions are not designed to say that you are not law abiding or not honest. They are asked to point out to you that the way we perceive ourselves is not always the way others may perceive us. If you set a value of honesty, then you need to make sure that we all understand what we mean by honesty.

As a leader, you may say that your people are important to you. What do you mean by important? If they perceive that being important means that you will listen to them, spend time with them and share your thoughts with them, then they will be very disappointed when you haven't got the time and you haven't told them something even though you were not in a position to tell them.

Be clear about your values and what you stand for. Be true to those values above all else. If you don't know them, then you can't expect your people to know them and you won't know if you are being true to them.

? How important is integrity and how much effort do you put into it?

Having integrity is very powerful. It takes a lot to win and not much too lose. Knowing what your values are and keeping to them is a major start to gaining integrity with people. Gaining it and keeping it should be two separate things that you need to work on.

One of the greatest ways to sustain integrity is to have the humility to acknowledge when you are wrong or have made a mistake. Once you have gained integrity with someone, it is very powerful because of the influence you have with that person. As with all power, there comes responsibility. Nothing damages integrity quicker than the person who abuses power. Cherish the integrity you have with someone and feed it, nurture it and be grateful for it. If you can manage this, then you won't lose it and waste the time that losing it will absorb.

? Are the people who you lead aware of the standards you expect from them?

There are two types of standards. One is the standards we expect in terms of the work being undertaken. These could include quality, timeliness, frequency or any other method of measuring the task or the product or service.

The other standard is about relationships. It is about code of conduct, behaviors or the values we share.

Both of these are important but often there is too much emphasis on the standards relating to the job. Not enough is given to the standards in terms of the accepted behaviors until it goes wrong and then we are in fix-it mode which is time consuming and costly.

From my experience, I have come to the conclusion that this is mainly for one of two reasons. The one reason is that the leaders have not defined the values or the acceptable code of conduct and so nothing is addressed until things are going wrong. The other reason is that the people in the position of leadership won't or can't personally live up to the values they have set. In this case, the leaders expect things of their people, but aren't prepared to always do it themselves.

? Are you a living, breathing personification of the values that you expect of others?

Are you consistent in the way that you deal with people? Once you are clear about your own values and have made people aware of the standards you expect of them, you can move on to being an example of the values you expect. You need to be the example to them that shows what *you* mean by these values, and shows them how to behave. In other words, you need to "walk the talk."

Consistency is a major part of this ability. We can all do something once in a while but that is not what is meant here. We are talking about being able to demonstrate it in a manner that shows that it is possible to do this all the time.

You are bound to have heard the expression "firm but fair." Remember, this has nothing to do with people liking you or even agreeing with you. It is about people knowing where they stand with you. You are a rock that they can always depend on and you will be unwavering in the manner you behave on particular issues of importance to them. It is about not having favorites that you let get away with some things or people that you pick on because you don't like them.

Values are something that you hold dear to you and you can be consistently relied on to be working within them.

? How good are you at dealing with people and building a lasting relationship?

This covers all of the above and a little more. At times, the leader needs to be firm and may even need to deal with conduct that is not acceptable or deal with a drop in performance. This requires straight talking, corrective action and even discipline on occasions.

A measure of how good you are in all of the above is the manner you can carry this out and maintain that person's motivation and their respect. If you have the level of integrity, if you have clear values, if you are perceived as firm but fair and if you are consistent in your behaviors, then you will be able to sustain the relationship and probably get them back on track.

When dealing with an issue, a leader is able to differentiate the behaviors from the person. When someone has done something wrong, the leader deals with the incorrect behavior and not how bad the person is. The leader also leaves the person clear on how to behave next time rather than dwelling on the mistake that was made. This refocusing on the future enables the relationship to move on and not dwell on the past.

People

? **How important are people to you and your organization?**

Remember that the mindset of a person will show itself in his or her behaviors. If you think that people are difficult and you need to manage them, then they will pick this up in your behaviors and respond accordingly.

The strength of your team, group or organization is as strong as the combined effort of the individuals in supporting each other. Facilitating the environment to allow this to take place is the principle function of a leader.

? **How good are you at listening?**

Listening is not simply about hearing the noise that arrives on your eardrums and then making sense of it. Listening is being able to understand what is being said and in some cases what is not said. Listening is about noticing actions, feeling the mood, seeing the situation for what it truly is and fully comprehending the real position or message that is trying to get through.

Too many people hear what is being said and don't get what is meant. They put their own interpretations on it and miss the essence of the message. They hear what they want to hear, notice what they want to notice and pay attention to the facts that prove their opinion or what they want to believe.

Good listening is the ability to suspend judgment and see things for what they really are, being prepared to use all the senses to receive information, and seeking the real situation and not just what people want you to believe. Most of all, good listening is about asking the right questions to be able to access the information needed.

The other aspect to listening is the ability to let people know that you have heard what they were saying. People want the recognition that you have noted what they have said. On the whole, people aren't stupid and know that you can't do everything and you can't change everything. However, they do want to know that you have taken on board their comments and have given them consideration or are investigated them. Simple acknowledgement that you have heard and considered what they have said is all most people want.

Notice how you feel, behave, look and act when someone is talking to you. I always remember one guy that used to look around the room when you talked to him. It was so frustrating and eventually I got to the stage that I would avoid having conversations with him. I found it amusing later to discover that many other people felt the same way about him. It was a great pity because he was a talented person but would never make a leader of people.

❓ How approachable are you?

A good measure of your people skills is the way people feel about approaching you. If you are not approachable, then there is something they are picking up about you that makes this a problem area for you.

I had to laugh recently when I visited a company and was told that when they have meetings, the staff never ask questions. The manager said this as though it was their fault for not asking. Having talked with the staff, I knew it was his fault for not being approachable and not creating the environment for them to be able to speak. They perceived this manager as not listening and having his own agenda which meant that it didn't matter what they said because he had already decided how it will be. Some very good people were being wasted by the lack of leadership that would bring out the best in them.

? How good are you at keeping people informed?

This is a difficult one because, many times in a position of leadership, you are not able to tell people everything for a variety or reasons. The point is do you tell them what you can?

Communication is a two way process which means that the responsibility is divided between both parties. One has to have the desire to communicate and the other needs to have the willingness to listen. A leader takes more than his or her responsibility for this process. In other words, taking responsibility for the giving of information as well as making sure that the information is received and understood. So this question is not about how good your systems are but how good are you at getting the message over so that people understand and know what to do with the information.

Nurturing

? How willing are you to learn?

A willingness to learn is the cornerstone to being a leader. A willingness to learn requires a frame of mind about learning that will propel forward at all times. This willingness to learn is not simply about studying, reading or research in terms of what you did at school and university. It is about being a "student of life" – learning all the time through watching, listening, having an open mind, being inquisitive and asking questions.

It is also about learning from mistakes and not justifying them. It is about seeing everything as a learning opportunity. It is a great step forward when you accept that mistakes are human nature but learning is what makes people people.

There is no right or wrong, there is only the opportunity to discover. A mistake can only be a mistake if you don't learn from it and then make it again. The willingness to learn requires two characteristics in particular. The first is the ability to ask the right question and the second is the sense to listen for the reply when it comes.

? How much time do you spend developing your knowledge and skills?

So you are willing to learn? How much time do you devote to it? Reading the daily paper and watching news channels or documentaries are not what is referred to here. I am not saying that these are not important but it is more than that.

Targeting subjects for investigation, getting details and knowledge about your market place, your industry, top performing people in this sector and anything else that will help you be more informed or make more informed judgments.

Someone once said to me that school was not there to give much in the way of information but rather to teach us how to learn. The older I get the more I appreciate how important that element is. I have met people who are learning for the sake of learning. Learning a new language, learning about a different country or learning about something in nature of the world that they have set their mind to.

I have referred to learning here as though it is a knowledge only requirement. This is not the case. Learning new skills is about learning also. Whether it is how to sky-dive, advance driving or using a computer, these skills are exercising the brain and helping increase the ability to lead people.

? How good are you at creating a learning culture in your team, group or organization?

Having mastered this ability in yourself, the next is the desire to do the same for your people. What do you do to help them develop themselves? Is learning a part of your culture? Blaming people is the opposite culture to a learning culture. Blame inhibits learning.

We are not talking about using an appraisal system. Appraisals (or the variety of names that organizations come up with these days) are all processes. They are a tool to help the novice leader and a structure to help ensue that the process is covered completely. A learning culture is an ongoing approach that changes the way we act. It is about the way we think. It is about who we are.

? How aware are you about future trends and developments in the marketplace?

I come across many managers who have good knowledge about their industry trends, market forces or political influences. A leader is aware of more then the obvious trends. A leader is aware of changing management thinking, of demographic changes, of next generation thinking and many more influences than the obvious.

More than just being aware of them, the leader is rising to the challenges and inventing them. Instead of being reactive the leader is proactive. Questions like:

If the whole market stopped buying our product tomorrow, what would they be buying instead?

If we were unable to produce what we do now, how would we still satisfy our customers' needs?

What will the next generation want from this industry when they no longer want to be like their parents?

and my favorite:

If we could add substantial value to the customer without raising overheads, how would we do it?

Some may think that these are impossible questions and other will say we are already asking these questions. Leaders are asking these and a thousand more questions. The secret is to ask the questions in as many different ways as possible to create more answers.

? How good are you at getting your team to think about future trends and developments in the marketplace?

All of the above applies to the team as much as to yourself. Leaders understand that their brains will never be as effective as the combined use of all the brains in the team or group. Leaders ask the same questions of their team and expect the team to ask the same questions, and more, of their leader and themselves.

Overview

? **How good are you at letting go?**

If you are learning, then are you moving on? If you have overview, then you no longer have personal control! The whole concept is about giving control while keeping ultimate responsibility. Responsibility is not about *having* control but *having* control is about taking responsibility.

Let me explain. As the leader, you are ultimately responsible for the actions of your team and the consequences of those actions. This does not mean that you control the people. If you control them, then you are not allowing them to think and you have shut down their ability to do so – you stunt progress.

What you do is let them control the system. However, to control the system they need to take responsibility.

The key to this working is that there are standards or systems in place to make sure that the job meets a certain standard. Having set the standard, the art of getting to 'overview' is getting the team to take responsibility for the systems or standards so that they control them.

Are you strong enough to let go of things even when you like doing them? Are you capable of recognizing when it is time for you to let go? I recently came across a managing director of a company employing 160 people with a turnover of $24m. He was personally opening the mail himself each morning! Asking him about this, his reply was, "I like to know what is going on!"

❓ What words would your people use to describe you?

Bearing in mind that you are a leader when people follow you, how would your people describe you in this context? Controller, manipulator, abdicator or supportive, hands-off approach, willing to let them have a go?

❓ Do you create the environment that allows empowerment to happen?

Is the purpose of your organization something that everyone understands? Are standards becoming the purpose or focus of their attention? How are people measured?

The structure of the organization is not a organization chart. Rather it is a way of ensuring that everyone recognizes the roles they play, the contributions they make and how the various systems help to achieve the purpose.

If anything in that structure is unclear, then the environment is not conducive to empowering and delegating to people. Check the measurements that you have in place and be sure that they are achieving what they should while at the same time motivating the people. If you are providing development for people, then check that it is working and people recognize the contribution it makes to the purpose of your organization.

❓ Are you prepared to help when they need it?

Last but not least, how good are you at providing the support people need to be motivated? Simple expectations can make the difference to many people.

Recently, I spoke to a man who was de-motivated because his line manager takes two months to process his appraisal documentation. Such a small matter that makes a huge difference in the performance of this person. What you think as insignificant may be very important to the people who work for you. It is often the little things that make a big difference and as a leader you need to be able to recognize them and act upon them accordingly.

Support is only as good as it is needed! If you think that what you do is supporting your team, then your assumption may be misplaced. Ask them how they want to be supported. A friend of mine took a new job recently and his new boss asked him, "How do you want to be managed?" (I would have preferred it if he had asked how he wanted to be led!) That conversation was so powerful in terms of gaining commitment and managing expectations.

Conclusion

I have not set out to provide the definitive answer to the subject of leadership. I set out to discover what makes a leader and found that as long as I live, I will discover new things about this subject.

I bow my head in respect to all the people before me, and those that will follow me with books and theories on this subject. We are all seeking something that enables us to understand. We want to know what makes the person that society so badly needs. We share a common interest although we have never met.

I have discovered that leadership starts from within. I have discovered that some principles need to be in place like the willingness to learn. I have discovered that integrity is so powerful that it has the ability to move people who don't even like you or agree with you. I discovered that empowerment is less to do with what you do and more to do with what your have in place. Most of all I learned that a leader is a person with a frame of mind that rules his or her behaviors.

I will continue my research and continue to work with organizations to help develop leaders for as long as I continue to have the success I have enjoyed to date.

I appeal to you to continue to do your own research and join me on this journey of discovery because it is …

a never-ending story … … …

Index

About the Author

Paul Bridle

Business Advisor, Trainer, Speaker and Personal Coach

Paul is a very motivational speaker and an outstanding trainer. He believes that people should go away from a sesion being able to put into practice what they have learnt. This makes Paul's presentations meaningful and beneficial to those who attend. Paul has successfully set up and run a number of companies and his work is now devoted to developing and training people to build successful organisations. As an outstanding trainer, he has been asked to run training sessions in a number of countries and is very popular in the UK.

Further information

Paul Bridle may be reached via the contact information below.

Proaction International, P O Box 14, Grantham, Lincolnshire, NG31 7BX, UK

Web: www.proaction-int.com
www.paulbridle.com